THE NAUTICAL INSTITUTE
PROJECT '93

International Conference and Workshops

ACCIDENT AND LOSS PREVENTION AT SEA

A

First published 1993 by The Nautical Institute,
202 Lambeth Road, London SE1 7LQ, UK.

Telephone: + 71 928 1351
Fax: + 71 401 2537

ISBN 1 870077 15 6

Although great care has been taken with the writing and production of this volume, neither The Nautical Institute nor the authors can accept any responsibility for errors, omissions or their consequences.

These papers have been prepared to address the subject of accident and loss prevention at sea. This should not, however, be taken to mean that this document deals comprehensively with all of the concerns which need to be addressed or even, where a particular matter is addressed, that this document sets out the only definitive view for all situations.

The opinions expressed are those of the authors only and are not necessarily to be taken as the policies or views of any organisation with which they have any connection.

Readers and students should make themselves aware of any local, national or international changes to bylaws, legislation, statutory and administrative requirements that have been introduced which might affect authors' conclusions.

CONTENTS

Typeset and printed in England by Silverdale Press, Silverdale Road, Hayes, Middlesex UB3 3BH.

Opening Address

WHY IS ACCIDENT PREVENTION SO SIGNIFICANT? WHY THIS CONFERENCE?

Captain L. A. Holder, ExC, MPhil, FNI, FCIT, FRIN

President, The Nautical Institute

Captain L. A. Holder

CAPTAIN HOLDER first went to sea with Alfred Holt and Co's Blue Funnel Line in 1953. He obtained his Master's Certificate in 1962 and Extra Master in 1963 at Liverpool College of Technology. From 1963 to 1965 Captain Holder was appointed warden of the Alfred Holt & Co cadet training establishment and then was appointed assistant lecturer at Liverpool Polytechnic Maritime Studies Department.

At Liverpool Polytechnic between 1972 and 1989 Captain Holder progressed to senior, then principal lecturer, being appointed head of department in 1977, and in 1988 Director of the Maritime and Engineering Faculty. Since 1989 Captain Holder has worked as an independent consultant.

Captain Holder obtained an MPhil by research on the subject of navigational accuracy in 1973 and is the author of a variety of research papers, some written independently and others co-jointly on subjects ranging from pilot training, VTS, technology and manning, and on-board training.

Amongst Captain Holder's current assignments is a project initiated by the Marine Society and supported by The Nautical Institute which is examining the potential for a credit accumulation scheme for mariners' qualifications.

Captain Holder has been connected with the Institute since its inception, having been involved with helping to draw up the Constitution. He was Chairman of the Papers and Technical Committee from 1972 to 1978 and is currently Chairman of the Institute's Education and Training Committee.

WHY IS ACCIDENT PREVENTION SO SIGNIFICANT? WHY THIS CONFERENCE?

Effect of accidents

MARITIME accidents affect people. A personal accident can affect a person's whole life, and the lives of his or her family. Being blamed for a major cargo claim can ruin a promising career and 'a collision at sea can spoil your whole day' is an often-quoted understatement which emphasises the need for good seamanship.

The costs and repercussions of major accidents spread outwards to other crew members, managers, emergency services, insurers, commercial interests and the public at large. The costs of ship repairs and disruption to services can usually be calculated, but the human costs are often immeasurable.

These concerns were expressed by members of The Nautical Institute responding to a survey initiated by the Council in 1992 to discover where the Institute could best direct its efforts to improve standards in the industry.

Evidence of a serious problem

Financial costs of accidents provide one source of evidence as to the extent of the problem. Direct commercial costs from navigational accidents are high, but pollution claims can multiply them. Cargo claims are also important. In one P&I Club there were 602 cargo claims totalling $235 million . . . and, significantly, 'more claims were caused by human error than by ship failure'. In the same *Analysis of Major Claims 1992*, the UK P&I Club reports, personal injury accidents were involved in '420 claims, totalling $145 million'. In the same year, the Liverpool and London P&I Club's claims manager reported that, for the first time, personal accident claims had exceeded cargo claims.

In addition to the analyses of claims, The Nautical Institute has started to collect and publish information on dangerous situations and near misses. Fortunately on these occasions no accident actually occurred. The International Marine Accident Reporting Scheme (MARS) is uncovering many situations where good fortune, rather than safe practices, prevented a major disaster.

Day-to-day contacts with members in all sectors of the industry have brought to light a large number of latent failures (dormant decisions or actions by designers, regulators and managers) which are awaiting the trigger by human error or omission at the sharp end to turn them into more accidents.

Personnel policies, human failings and motivation

Internationalisation of the industry has made the communication of policies and ideas more difficult, through barriers of language and culture. Changes in the way personnel are recruited, trained and appointed often distance senior managers from sea-farers.

The term 'human error' above is defined as 'any human action or omission identifiable as the immediate cause of the event from which the liability arises'. Instances cited have involved not only a lack of knowledge or experience, but simple human failings such as pride, misunderstandings, confusion, fatigue, errors in calculations, distractions or moods, etc. Behavioural science is a complex subject and there are no easy solutions.

Role of The Nautical Institute

The Nautical Institute is neither a trade association nor a trade union. It is an independent and impartial organisation and is in a position to initiate ideas and practices which can be of considerable benefit to companies and to the seafarers they employ.

Cultures and backgrounds

It is apparent to the Institute that poor attitudes to personal welfare and safety are indicative of low morale and are likely to be reflected in poor attitudes to the safety of the ship and its cargo. Error-free operations can be provided only by a work force with confidence, high personal esteem and a corresponding minimum of personal accidents.

When the Nautical Institute published *The Management of Safety in Shipping*, the final summing up highlighted the importance and complexity of attitudes to safety:

> . . . *attitudes to safety by those who work within an industry are affected by culture, training and certification, experience, conditions of employment, personal ambitions, company style, regulatory frameworks, the ability of crews to work together and many other factors which relate to commercial operations.*

Accident prevention should be regarded as a valuable and essential aspect of industrial development, saving costs and contributing to enduring commercial and personal success. It comes about through teamwork between all the personnel involved ashore and afloat.

Regulatory approaches

Rules and regulations provide a necessary framework for commercial operations. However, trying to reduce accidents solely by imposing and enforcing more and more regulations will, beyond a certain point, become less effective. It will follow a law of diminishing returns. Those at the sharp end eventually take a cynical view of the growing deluge of convention clauses, resolutions, recommendations, shipping notices, company instructions and dire warnings. They will regard the army of supervisors, surveyors, inspectors and quality assurance consultants, not as a task force helping them to

AA

improve safety, but as instruments to effect control through the medium of regulations and to limit institutional liability in the event of an accident—a biased jury to convict them if they fail.

Education and training

Some accidents may be the result of ignorance due to poor basic training, but many more appear to be brought about through poor attitudes to work and safety. It is important that personnel in the industry are properly trained in the basic principles and practices of ship and port operations, with great emphasis on safe procedures. There is scope for improvement in the shore-based courses and in practical sea-training, but, as with regulation, this alone will not stop latent failures turning into accidents.

A safety culture

Reduction of accidents and losses can come only from a safety culture which starts with top managers and is reflected right through to the attitude of those at the sharp end of operations.

Company cultures are important. Companies such as Shell, Chevron and Mobil have built personal accident prevention into their safety policies as a matter of priority, and the task to which the Institute can contribute is the spreading of awareness concerning the significance of personal attitudes towards accident prevention.

On any ship, and in any company, the problem cannot be tackled in isolation. The most important influence is the safety policy, commitment to implementation and the continued visible interest and monitoring by senior management ashore (and

afloat). Essential too, is the positive attitude to safety of personnel on board, at much greater arm's length from senior managers than in any other industry, who must be convinced that good working practices are worth striving for, so supporting initiatives from the sea.

Aims of this Conference and Workshop

The Nautical Institute is international, and its strength lies in the membership, particularly in the branches, where the world scene can be put into local perspective and positive actions initiated. During this Conference, three experienced speakers will give their views and then invite participants to identify local issues and discuss steps which can be taken to improve safety and reduce accidents.

On behalf of The Nautical Institute, I wish you success in today's efforts to help all concerned to create a climate in which accidents, particularly those caused by human error, are reduced.☐

Useful references

1992   *Analysis of Claims 1992.* The United Kingdom Mutual Steam Ship Assurance Association (Bermuda) Limited.

1992   International Marine Accident Reporting Scheme (MARS). Results published regularly in *Seaways.* Journal of the Nautical Institute.

1991   *The Management of Safety in Shipping.* A Nautical Institute publication on operations and quality assurance.

1992/3 'The Importance of Personal Health and Safety Training. (A Pro-active Approach to Zero Accidents).' A paper by Captain P. C. Dyer, MNI. *Seaways* June 1993.

FLEET MANAGEMENT WHAT IS ITS ROLE IN ACCIDENT PREVENTION?

Captain A. T. Thompson, MNI
Formerly Senior Marine Adviser, Chevron Shipping Company

Captain A.T. Thompson

CAPTAIN ALEC THOMPSON commenced his sea training in 1948 and has been associated with the marine/transportation side of the oil industry ever since, having served at sea in various capacities from Apprentice to Master and ashore as tug Master and marine Pilot before moving into marine operations/administration.

His experience includes an involvement with scheduling, programming and chartering of tankers, fleet operations management, including safety, administration and marine terminal management.

In 1974, Captain Thompson was seconded to the Oil Companies International Marine Forum (OCIMF) as a technical advisor for a period of three years; during the secondment he was closely involved with the work of the International Maritime Organization, the International Chamber of Shipping and other national and international bodies.

During his time in San Francisco, he was a founding member and first Chairman of the West Coast USA Branch of The Nautical Institute in 1990. He remained Chairman until just before his departure from the USA.

His last appointment was as Senior Marine Advisor to Chevron Shipping Company and was based in San Francisco, California.

FLEET MANAGEMENT WHAT IS ITS ROLE IN ACCIDENT PREVENTION?

AS 1993 DRAWS TO A CLOSE, it appears that the shipping industry will survive yet another year and be prepared to meet the challenges of the upcoming year. These challenges will again be legislative, economic, financial, *et al*, but one of the biggest challenges will still be how to keep our personnel and vessels free of accidents and incidents.

Our industry is extremely diverse in the number of types of vessels and trades we are involved with, but the commonality throughout is the people, the vessel and working in the same medium. Equally diverse are the types of management, whether hands-on or other, but one common trait is required both ashore and afloat and that is full commitment to safe operations at all times. How long will it be before we genuinely accept that safety is good business?

Over the last 20 years we have gone from a surplus of traditional seafarers in general and officers in particular to a shortage of high quality personnel at all levels. To overcome this shortage of traditional personnel many companies turned to other areas to meet their needs, which immediately led to creating an area of potential conflict with the national shipowners of these countries and, if the experts are to be believed, has created or will create even greater shortages by the beginning of the next century. The use of lower-cost personnel from non-traditional seafaring nations has been a straw to clutch at for many ship operators who have tried to reduce direct operating costs in the short term in order to compensate for the generally lower freight rates over the preceding years.

Some of those who chose not to use alternative crews, whether voluntarily or involuntarily, often turned to reducing crew size to keep the operating costs down. If shipping companies cannot make money from shipping operations, where do they raise capital to finance new tonnage—who wants to invest money in a losing operation?

In the tanker industry, the introduction of OPA 90 in the aftermath of the *Exxon Valdez* incident has led to new requirements being laid on tanker operators/owners: strict limited working hour requirements; individual vessel contingency plans which in many instances require to be approved also by individual coastal States; double hulls; establishment of clean-up organisations around the coasts; tug escorts, etc.; additional training; numerous inspections by numerous organisations; vapour recovery from cargo tanks where the atmosphere is being displaced; and so on.

Quality overall

About the same time as OPA 90 came along, some of the shipping companies' shore establishments were hearing about quality—total quality improvement (TQI)—continuous quality improvement (CQI)—Malcolm Baldridge concepts—ISO 9000—BS 5750, etc. Could this be the vehicle to help management

eliminate some of the personnel accidents and incidents—so many of the concepts were the same—reviewing each operation before commencement—doing it right the first time—using only good materials and tools—avoiding waste—eliminating errors—ensuring good working environments. Application of quality concepts can and will lead to a reduction in all accidents including personnel, but our goal should, at all times, be zero accidents and/or incidents.

Quality in the basic sense is all the things our mother tried to instil in us while growing up: 'If you are going to do a job, do it right'; or 'Do it right the first time or not at all'. In the more formal sense 'Quality is meeting or exceeding the expectation of the customer'. For many years most seafarers have tried to run a quality operation before it was given the name of ISO 9000 series or BS 5750—delivering the entrusted cargo in the same condition as received was always the end objective—obeying your own flag or country rules even though nobody was there to check you and violations would not be detected.

Now, in an era of 'bottom lining' all our operations, it is essential to ensure that we do not make mistakes, particularly avoidable ones, as this means we must correct the mistake which in turn costs money. Good basic training plus training by example and hands-on will become more and more essential as ageing fleets will require experienced and competent seafarers to maintain them to national and international current standards. Operators who suffer accidents through failing to maintain and operate their vessels effectively will find the cost of such accidents prohibitive.

In a study carried out by the BP Tanker Company over a 20-year period and 1,600 ship-years of operation, the following pattern emerged in order of priority by cost:

1. Machinery and structural damage.

2. Fire and explosion.

3. Collisions (447 recorded).

4. Groundings.

5. Contact with docks.

6. Weather and ice damage.

7. Damage of unknown origin.

8. Foundering.

During the period, 50 lives were lost; 75 per cent of the 6,000 incidents had no cost recorded against them as they fell below the prevailing insurance deductible or P&I franchise and could not be recovered[1]. When considering the economic implications of incidents, it is interesting to study the breakdown of numbers of claims when compared with the cost of the claims. Figures provided by the Central Union of Norwegian Underwriters show this comparison. When developing an accident prevention programme priority can be given to those areas which give rise to the highest

Table 1 shows breakdown of all claims per type of casualty as aggregated total for the years 1988-91

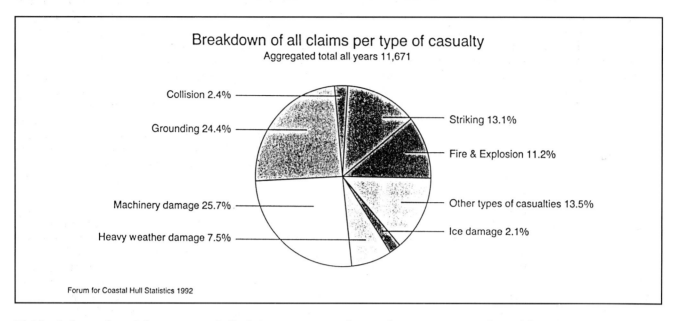

Breakdown of all claims per type of casualty
Aggregated total all years 11,671

Collision 2.4%
Grounding 24.4%
Machinery damage 25.7%
Heavy weather damage 7.5%
Striking 13.1%
Fire & Explosion 11.2%
Other types of casualties 13.5%
Ice damage 2.1%

Forum for Coastal Hull Statistics 1992

Table 2 shows breakdown cost of all claims per type of casualty as aggregated total for the years 1988-91

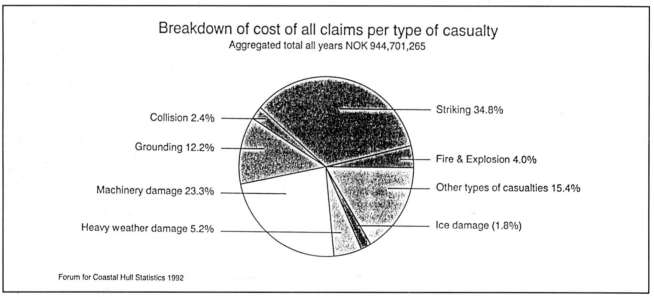

Breakdown of cost of all claims per type of casualty
Aggregated total all years NOK 944,701,265

Collision 2.4%
Grounding 12.2%
Machinery damage 23.3%
Heavy weather damage 5.2%
Striking 34.8%
Fire & Explosion 4.0%
Other types of casualties 15.4%
Ice damage (1.8%)

Forum for Coastal Hull Statistics 1992

claims. Accidents, however, are not predictable and the overall aim must be to eliminate them altogether.

Eliminating waste

The application of CQI will bring its own rewards in that waste will be eliminated or, at least, minimised; therefore profits will increase because we are avoiding the waste—whether material, time or processes. This concept does, however, require the management to be committed to the process as quality comes down from the top—not in a trickle but with full, viable commitment. In its early stages taking on quality activities and concepts can be disruptive, especially in the more procedurally-bound companies, as teams require to be formed to start the process of change. These teams should be cross-functional, as teams of the same discipline tend to solve their problems but compound other parties' problems.

A company which elects to enter the quality process has to ensure that all its employees are trained at appropriate levels in quality. This cannot be accomplished at the stroke of a pen, but with good communications those who are trained later rather than earlier can be kept aware and involved throughout. It is essential that the personnel at the highest levels of the company are trained first in order that all employees can see the commitment from the top.

Shipping companies used to be 'us and them' type operations, but in recent years great efforts have been made to move this barrier (another quality process we did not recognise!) wherein the ship and shore recognise each other's skills to the benefit of both groups. If the ship and shore work together as a team mutually supporting each other, great improvements can be made—but they must communicate openly with each other at all times.

Data for data's sake

Collecting data for the sake of collecting is demoralising to those who are required to do the collecting, and computers now enable us to collect data at a rate never envisaged years ago. Efficient programmes developed specifically for measuring quality can be of great assistance in identifying problem areas and thereby allowing solutions to be developed. In the quality process there are hard and soft measures; the former is the physical counting of objects, processes, people, etc., and comparing them to previous or later counts. Soft measures are more intangible and are the feelings, perceptions, views, etc., of people which can be compared on a mathematical basis—e.g., confidential surveys of people, results of focus groups, and so on.

By truly working as a team both ship and shore representatives can effectively make positive changes as a consequence of identifying genuine problem areas. A quick overview by the supervisor at whatever level will not always identify the real problem, especially if we are consciously or unconsciously biased in the review. Pareto chart process will tend to show that 80 per cent of the problems encountered are caused by the same 20 per cent of processes—that 80 per cent of the calls you receive will be from the same 20 per cent of callers.

We can use flowcharting to set down how various (or numerous) stages take us from start to end of a process and what or where safeguards are in position, but then we can see if the process is still meeting its objective today—e.g., requisitioning stores/spare parts, delivery of spares, and so on.

An example of this is a big manufacturing company which over the years processed invoices for goods supplied to other people. The time to process an invoice was 42 days, because as the company grew it just kept adapting/adding on and employing more people to handle the flow. As a result of the quality process, it now handles the process in $3\frac{1}{2}$ hours. This required investment in modern information transfer equipment, and the surplus people were trained into other functions. All this may seem to be divorced from safety, but (as it was noted earlier) quality and safety have a lot of common ground.

All the quality systems have the same goal—standard process/procedures to ensure conformity and consistency in the way business is conducted—including our own. The *IMO Management Code* can set the minimum level desired, but until administration accept and adapt the code as the minimum level for that fleet it just remains a document. Nothing prevents an administration from requiring higher levels for their own vessels once they have accepted the code as is. Such a procedure ensures that all vessels will meet a worldwide defined common standard, but does not inhibit national progress with their own vessels. (See Annex 1.)

Responsible and accountable management

The role of management over the recent years has become more specifically defined in that it has always been responsible to its own board of directors for the safe, economic, efficient operation of its vessels, but now is also being made accountable to society for its failures, of whatever nature, to whatever degree. The *Herald of Free Enterprise* and *Exxon Valdez* cases are recent examples of this accountability. Management now has to ensure that it has fully trained personnel at all levels, well maintained vessels, up-to-date manual systems for operations, engineering, good communications, competent knowledgeable recruiting departments, and motivated safety personnel.

Shore management have to be seen to be an integral part of the whole operation, giving clear direction by quality communications to the seagoing personnel, preferably in person, encouraging feedback from all levels of the company. Shipboard management teams are successful when both ship and shore make a full commitment to the process. Who better to know what the vessel requires to do its job than the people who have the job to do?

When information is openly and honestly exchanged between the ship and shore, then realistic estimates of costs can be made regarding operations and future repairs and maintenance requirements. The shipboard management can monitor its own progress and control storing requirements, when to make repairs/overhauls/routine maintenance, etc., and be both responsible and accountable. Up to the middle of the last century vessels usually managed themselves for long periods and overall this was reasonably successful.

People must be seen as individuals who can contribute to the welfare and progress of the company, and if unmotivated can be the cause of the demise or serious deterioration of the company finances. In the present and future environmentally aware world in which we trade, management will require to have in place good shipboard/shoreside contingency plans to meet the requirements of the trading pattern of its vessels. The plan will require to be critiqued and continually updated, and tested out frequently. Familiarity with the plan will ensure that if an emergency does develop the incident will be efficiently handled and accidents with unusual equipment and situations will be minimised. Failure to have realistic, updated plans is false economy as it will save money in the short term only.

Working as a team

Shore management teams usually include operational, engineering, commercial, financial, legal, human resources and safety as each is reliant upon each other for the successful operation of the vessels and company. A well-equipped vessel with a fully trained crew is not of much use if it has no trade; conversely, a good trip charter is to no avail if the engines do not work. All groups are interdependent and must work as a team. In the era of low freights the pressure to reduce costs of operating (in the total sense) is extremely high and the danger is created of having short-term solutions to long-term problems based on the belief that if today's profits are not produced then there will not be a tomorrow!

In hard times, safety and training are often minimised or even eliminated because the results of good safety and training programmes are hard to quantify in real money terms; but, after a fairly short time, the results of bad programmes are easy to see and quantify. The question is often asked; 'Why do we need safety personnel if we have a good safety record?'; or 'Why do we need to train? Isn't that their responsibility?' Could it be the good safety record is because there is a safety programme?

Management, therefore, has to balance the various components involved to meet its objectives of safe, economic, efficient operations and to make hard decisions when fine-tuning the budget. Safety and training should be an important part of the budget process and should be viewed as being as necessary as bunkers. Frequently the shipboard personnel can be of great assistance in using their specific knowledge and skills to make proposals to assist in minimising costs and should therefore be fully consulted within the quality process.

In the employment of its seagoing personnel, it is necessary for the company to set the minimum standards of qualifications required to join and to ensure that personnel already serving with them are appraised of their career path within the company. People generally wish to feel they are an integral part of an organisation—not merely a number or resource pulled out in time of need—and if that positive environment can be established, individuals will give that little extra. Shipboard personnel are ambassadors of the company and their actions and the actions of the ship can influence business activities, so encouraging loyalty to the company can have positive financial results.

Long-service benefit

From a safety perspective, long-term seafarers have been shown to be less prone to accidents, and new employees suffer a high number of accidents due to improper attention/actions. Training in safety matters is essential, and mandatory courses plus company courses plus on-board training by appropriate training/safety personnel can be highly beneficial.

Having good terms of employment, particularly length of on-board duty plus receiving at least 85 per cent vacation due each time, is necessary if personnel are to be fully rested before returning to their chosen occupation. Visits to home office (head office) for senior personnel as a minimum are vital if the true team philosophy is to be effective—preferably on the way to vacation as problems are then still real. Continuing to employ and utilise long-term personnel is financially good business too as it avoids people passing through the dangerous first-year employee accident zone which helps to keep the safety incidents down.

Guidance from operational manuals

The issuance of manuals to vessels can be of great assistance to the shipboard personnel, but management must be aware of the contents and ensure that their shipboard personnel at all levels are aware of, and have access to, the manuals. Senior shipboard and office personnel should be very familiar with the manuals and ensure that they are used appropriately. For a fuller appreciation of operating and safety manuals and plans see the paper by C. R. Cushing in the book *The Management of Safety in Shipping*[2].

It may be well to note the old axiom 'Rules are made for the guidance of wise men and the blind obedience of fools'—this is so with operational manuals, as they are to provide the master and his staff with guidance gained from experience learned, possibly painfully, over the intervening years. Within the quality process operating manuals are essential; however, it is well to ensure that your current manuals are indeed the way you work and not the way the company believes it works! A shipboard library of business books, manuals, International Maritime Organization publications, administrations mandatory manuals, Oil Companies International Marine Forum and International Chamber of Shipping (plus the Society of International Gas Tanker & Terminal Operators, *et al*) is vital if the vessel is to conduct its business in compliance with the law—costly, yes, but cheap to ensure being in compliance and, if the shipboard personnel are high calibre professionals, they will use such books at all times.

Management require the vessel to be in compliance at all times, but periodically they will require to reaffirm the commitment of the company to full compliance—management should be seen to be active and not just making the correct noise. One method to achieve this is the establishment of a strong superintendent's programme, comprised of knowledgeable professional understanding individuals who have served as a master or chief engineer, preferably in the current fleet. These individuals will be the top of the quality rated senior individuals who will ride the vessel evaluating, observing, guiding, counselling, training, carrying out investigations when necessary, but supporting the master and shipboard personnel in meeting the company's objectives while ensuring full compliance with the laws of the vessel/country or both at all times.

The superintendents, to be fully effective, should be middle management and seen to be an extension of the fleet manager's office, having that authority when carrying out their duties, and will report in to the company at senior management level. Such high-level exposure will ensure that the messages, whether from the vessels or from the shore, are authentic and will tend to eliminate some of the scepticism which can be found between the ship and shore. Superintendents can review potential candidates for promotion, evaluate performance of personnel, specifically senior individuals, and make recommendations to the senior management for recognition awards for outstanding individuals. Major changes of policy can be carried to the vessels, thus ensuring the shipboard people can have the opportunity to discuss the background and/or their concerns with a senior management representative. Superintendents can liaise with shore terminals to ensure problems are handled promptly and that positive feedback is given to the terminal where appropriate.

Input to newbuilding programmes through the superintendents ensures that first-class avenues of communications are available to the shipboard personnel, designs of new jetties can incorporate users' ideas, etc. Quality techniques can also be received and updated through superintendents' visits.

Safety

In our highly competitive industry, managers for owners/operators are required to be cost conscious at all times. However, the problem can be that short-term financial gains develop into long-term problems both in material and finanaces. Ensuring that safety is maintained and equipment remains reliable at all times can initially appear to be expensive but, compared to having an accident, such costs pale into insignificance. Extending the operating life of machinery overhauls by simply delaying the overhaul can lead to accidents and to the vessel being unable to operate when it is required.

Risk management, which is the art of comparing the probability and severity of a casualty to the cost of preventing it, has been used extensively over the years but gets honed up in periods of low or no profits and may lead to curtailing safety training activities. Various industry figures available indicate that the cost of personnel accidents run between US$12,000 and US$34,000 per incident. However, it could be even higher, as some companies in earlier years only accounted for the direct cost to the injured and not the consequential costs to the operation overall, plus third parties.

There is no doubt that a well-constructed safety awareness and accident prevention programme brings results. The analysis conducted by Chevron Shipping Co. demonstrates that there is a relationship between a good safety culture and accident prevention. This is verified in two ways.

First, when new employees are taken on by the company, they typically suffer 33 injuries (mostly minor) during their first year of employment. This reduces to 10 in their third year and after five years reduces to just three where it remains. The company wishes to bring the figure to zero.

Since Chevron introduced its fleet safety policy, the injury rate in the fleet has gone down from 1.8 per 200,000 man-hours in 1972 to 0.8 in 1992, which is a significant achievement. The accident rate is continuing to diminish and this emphasises the need for long term commitment to steady improvement.

Tired machinery and/or individuals failing during their work time, and untrained workers in sensitive jobs can also be very expensive. For example, oil escaping from the vessel cargo system into the environment can cost up to US$80,000 per barrel to clean up, depending where the incident took place, time of the year, time of day and type of oil. Such a cost would be based on a highly sensitive environmental area, late night Christmas night/New Year's Eve/national holiday, strong tidal flow waterway, proximity to expensive marinas, etc.

Dangers of false economy

To minimise or eliminate the exposure to these incidents, training of people and safety awareness require to be maintained and the dangers of false economy have to be recognised as it is apparent that accidents to people at an average of US$23,000 and oil at US$40,000 per barrel spilled cannot be sustained. Additionally, there is the damaged reputation that comes to an accident-prone company and the market for the company may be damaged or destroyed.

Accidents involving the vessel physically vary from a rope in the propeller to striking third party property with death involved. Even the smallest of accidents to a foreign trading vessel will result in costs in excess of US$20,000 with lost time for survey reports, issuing seaworthiness or fitness to proceed, plus communications throughout and usually much more. With costs in the area of the foregoing it should be apparent that a training commitment from management is only good business.

Maintaining training

Ongoing improvement can be undertaken in most fleets by a commitment from the management to maintaining training in excess of that required mandatorially, maintaining and being visibly supportive of superintendency and safety programmes, ensuring that maintenance of the vessel and equipment are undertaken in a responsible way rather than decreeing that all will be well after extending the running periods, deferring overhauls, etc. The quality process, through brainstorming, cause of effect, flow charting, etc., will permit review of options, costs, risks, and so on, and by those processes the priorities can be presented and responsible decisions made which will ensure the viability of a continued operation.

Developing a safe operation policy which can be displayed on special notice boards on each vessel and on each floor of the shoreside offices can be beneficial by keeping safety prominently in view daily. These boards also show the realistic target set for the current year (zero will be the ultimate) and each month reflects the lack (or otherwise) of accidents per vessel and also for the fleet; similarly for the offices. Procedures should be established wherein every accident or incident receives the full glare of management attention. The system will require carefully considered definitions and procedures to be established for reporting —e.g., first aid, non-lost time, lost time, etc.—responsibilities identified for all personnel and well known reward/recognition programmes.

In Annex II Chevron has a procedure for accident investigation which does not end with finding out about the facts. It ends up with concrete recommendations for the prevention of repeat accidents.

On an annual basis, or other agreed period, all those who have been accident free should be eligible for recognition or reward. Various levels of awards can be established to reflect the different levels of responsibility experienced. The number of awards should be only a proportion of the potential winners to ensure continued competition—the actual winners will be drawn from those eligible. Identifying and establishing goals can help to focus people's commitment as can bench marking. Bench marking is a goal setting process wherein an achievement setting recognised company is selected and directing efforts to beat that selected company's goals in specific fields or categories. It may also be appropriate that all employees are cognisant of the fact that safety is an element under review when candidates for promotion are considered and therefore, unsafe operations and acts can be hazardous to career progress.

Owners/operators who are committed to good quality training and safety processes and who can show a low accident rate for both people and vessel should emphasise this with their P&I Clubs. A reduction in rates can usually be negotiated if it can be shown the risk to the Club is considerably less than other clients. Such reduction is to the benefit of the bottom line and one of the goals is to minimise operating costs. For those companies not represented on the boards of P&I Clubs, meetings with the Clubs on a regular basis helps each side to understand the efforts and direction of the other and, in times of need may remove some of the potential for misunderstanding.

Environmental awareness

In the same way that training and safety can suffer in hard economic times so, too, with environmental protection. Protecting the environment has always been good business, but even more important is that damaging the environment can be very bad business both from an image and financial perspective. It is essential that management continues to re-affirm its commitment to good safe practices to minimise or eliminate mistakes. Junior staff have to know that there is only one way to do the job and that is the safe, correct way. Senior staff need to be assured that they will be supported by management when they incur delay as a consequence of exercising an option which did not put the environment at risk.

In some cases accidents which take place are caused by putting financial gain ahead of environmental protection, carrying out the more risky concurrent operations (without inbuilt safeguards) because the consecutive operation would have taken a little more time (but not so risky). Saving expense by not sending a person on a non-mandatory training course who then has an accident damaging to the environment— the cost of any of these bad decisions is many more times expensive than the money which was originally 'saved'. In these situations management should not ask the question 'Can we afford to do it?' but rather 'Can we afford not to do it?'.

The application of OPA 90 (Oil Pollution Act 1990) to oil tankers in the waters of the USA has led to owners/operators reviewing their tanker operations, especially in light of the new liability laws which can potentially cause an owner/operator to be exposed to unlimited liability. Some owners/operators have compared the potential profit of the voyage against the potential cost in the case of an incident and have elected not to carry USA-bound cargoes. Vessels may meet all the latest requirements of IMO but to no avail if pollution results, as the regulations/laws, if fully applied, could spell the demise of, or serious financial loss to the company. Even in a high market the profit for the trip may be unattractive when compared to the financial consequences of an incident leading to environmental pollution.

Owners/operators will require to ensure that all mandatory requirements and obligations are being fulfilled at all times; that maintenance is not only good but the past records will bear scrutiny and confirm a high standard has been maintained; and that class surveys have been carried out as required and all recommendations complied with in all cases. As IMO

gathers momentum in its further efforts to increase the safety of seafarers and minimise pollution it can be anticipated that inspections will become more prolific than at present, and further that port States will take a harder line before allowing violators to sail.

Delays to vessels for infringements of laws and regulations will cost money and, although these costs may initially be recovered from the P&I Clubs, membership costs of the Clubs will rise and/or additional calls will be made on members to cover the additional outgoings. To maintain reasonable costs it is believed that the Clubs will then identify those with continuous claims for violations and initially charge higher premiums and then as a final move will refuse to give the cover due to the ongoing avoidable risks. Alternatively, good owners/operators can leave the Club which continues to cover poor operators and apply to join Clubs which recognise good quality performers.

Concluding overview

When markets are low, the shipboard and shore management teams will require to work effectively as a unified team and using quality processes endeavour to establish areas of lost time, duplication of processes/effort and potential waste, prioritise requirements, operations, etc. Many areas will be found which can be improved by planning events and not 'shooting from the hip'. It is a truism that the time can always be found to do the job correctly the second time although there wasn't the time to to it right the first time.

Effectively planning the vessel's operations and the use of personnel requires everybody to then be familiar with the plan and each to review their own participation. Entering and leaving port and port duties are usually heavy work load periods, but careful planning with back ups/alternatives identified can help to minimise the exposure to overwork. Accidents occur more frequently when personnel are tired, and continuous tiredness can lead to fatigue and its consequences.

Sailing when watchkeepers are tired or fatigued can lead to costly accidents but owners/operators in general appear to be reluctant to hold their vessels for eight/twelve hours to allow the personnel to rest. A delay of that magnitude can cost in general terms in a high market around US$12,000-14,000 but a minor soft grounding or brushing collision will be US$20,000 plus; a low market could be US$6,000-7,000 but repair costs will be the same. It would therefore appear to be good business to give serious consideration to rest the shipboard personnel. If the vessel is on an extremely tight schedule and management cannot 'afford' the time, it may be that the manning roster for the run should be reviewed. Accidents are not cost-effective ways of doing business and must be reduced with a goal of zero.

Public concern for the safety of the environment can lead to political activities and involvement which may mean political solutions for operational accidents and their consequences—this is already happening in some countries of the world. In turn this will usually increase the cost of operations without a commensurate increase in freight rates/revenues. Such a scenario should be an incentive to the industry, particularly management to run a quality operation where the finances can be controlled by the business, and not have heavy costs imposed by other parties.

The marine industry has always risen to meet the challenges of the day and the end of the 20th century challenges are but another opportunity where the industry can demonstrate its commitment to the safety of individuals, a safe environment and accident-free quality operations. The cost of doing it any other way is not acceptable.☐

References

1. 'The Broad Operational Scene and its Management.' R. Maybourn. *Proceedings of the Conference on Safety at Sea and in the Air*—Royal Aeronautical Society 1990.

2. *The Management of Safety in Shipping*. The Nautical Institute 1990.

ANNEX 1

1. DRAFT PROPOSALS FOR THE IMO SHIP MANAGEMENT CODE

1.2 OBJECTIVES

1.2.1 The objectives of the Code are to ensure safety at sea, prevention of human injury or loss of life, and avoidance of damage to the environment, in particular, to the marine environment, and to property.

1.2.2 Safety management objectives of the company should, *inter alia*: provide for safe practices in ship operation and a safe working environment; establish safeguards against all identified risks; and continuously improve safety management skills of personnel ashore and aboard ships, including preparing for emergencies related both to safety and environmental protection.

1.2.3 The safety and management system should ensure: compliance with mandatory rules and regulations; and that applicable codes, guidelines and standards recommended by the IMO, administrations, classification societies and maritime industry organisations are taken into account.

1.3 APPLICATION

The requirements of this Code may be applied to all ships.

1.4 Functional requirements for a Safety Management System (SMS)

Every company should develop, implement and maintain a Safety Management System (SMS) which includes the following functional requirements: a safety and environmental protection policy; instructions and procedures to ensure safe operation of ships and protection of the environment in compliance with relevant international and flag State legislation; defined levels of authority and lines of communication between, and amongst, shore and shipboard personnel; procedures for reporting accidents and non-conformities with the provisions of this Code; procedures to prepare for and respond to emergency situations; and procedures for internal audits and management reviews.

2. SAFETY AND ENVIRONMENTAL PROTECTION POLICY

2.1 The company should establish a safety and environmental protection policy which describes how the objectives, given in paragraph 1.2, will be achieved.

2.2 The company should ensure that the policy is implemented and maintained at all levels of the organisation, both ship based as well as shore based.

3. COMPANY RESPONSIBILITIES AND AUTHORITY

3.1 If the entity who is responsible for the operation of the ship is other than the owner, the owner must report the full name and details of such entity to the administration.

3.2 The company should define and document the responsibility, authority and interrelation of all personnel who manage, perform and verify work relating to and affecting safety and pollution prevention.

3.3 The company is responsible for ensuring that adequate resources and shore-based support are provided to enable the designated person or persons to carry out their functions.

4. DESIGNATED PERSON(S)

To ensure the safe operation of each ship and to provide a link between the company and those on board, every company, as appropriate, should designate a person or persons ashore having direct access to the highest level of management. The responsibility and authority of the designated person or persons should include monitoring the safety and pollution prevention aspects of the operation of each ship and to ensure that adequate resources and shore-based support are applied, as required.

5. MASTER'S RESPONSIBILITY AND AUTHORITY

5.1 The company should clearly define and document the master's responsibility with regard to: implementing the safety and environmental protection policy of the company; motivating the crew in the observation of that policy; issuing appropriate orders and instructions in a clear and simple manner; verifying that specified requirements are observed; and reviewing the SMS and reporting its deficiencies to the shore-based management.

All compliant

Wrong motivation, or Master-
Leading crew

5.2 The company should ensure that the SMS operating on board the ship contains a clear statement emphasising the master's authority. The company should establish in the SMS that the master has the overriding authority and the responsibility to make decisions with respect to safety and pollution prevention and to request the company's assistance as may be necessary.

6. RESOURCES AND PERSONNEL

6.1 The company should ensure that the master is: properly qualified for command; fully conversant with the company's SMS; and given the necessary support to that the master's duties can be safely performed.

6.2 The company should ensure that each ship is manned with qualified, certificated and medically fit seafarers in accordance with national and international requirements.

6.3 The company should establish procedures to ensure that new personnel and personnel transferred to new assignments related to safety and protection of the environment are given proper familiarisation with their duties. Instructions which are essential to be provided prior to sailing should be identified, document and given.

6.4 The company should ensure that all personnel involved in the company's SMS have an adequate understanding of relevant rules, regulations, codes and guidelines.

6.5 The company should establish and maintain procedures for identifying any training which may be required in support of the SMS and ensure that such training is provided for all personnel concerned.

6.6 The company should establish procedures by which the ship's personnel receive relevant information on the SMS in a working language or languages understood by them.

6.7 The company should ensure that the ship's personnel are able to communicate effectively in the execution of their duties related to the SMS.

7. DEVELOPMENT OF PLANS FOR SHIPBOARD OPERATIONS

The company should establish procedures for the preparation of plans and instructions for key shipboard operations concerning the safety of the ship and the prevention of pollution. The various tasks involved should be defined and assigned to qualified personnel.

8. EMERGENCY PREPAREDNESS

8.1 The company should establish procedures to identify, describe and respond to potential emergency shipboard situations.

8.2 The company should establish programmes for drills and exercises to prepare for emergency actions.

8.3 The SMS should provide for measures ensuring that the company's organisation can respond at any time to hazards, accidents and emergency situations involving its ships.□

Annex II

NAVIGATIONAL AND SEAMANSHIP INCIDENTS— COULD THEY HAVE BEEN AVOIDED?

Mr C.J. Parker, BSc, FNI
Secretary, The Nautical Institute

B

Mr. C.J. Parker

JULIAN PARKER obtained his Master's Foreign-Going Certificate in 1967, having served in cargo ships and tankers in various ranks. He then obtained a BSc in nautical science at Liverpool Polytechnic, studying naval architecture, marine engineering and control systems.

In 1970 he was appointed Administrative Staff Training Officer of the Ocean Group, Britain's second largest shipping company. During this appointment, Mr Parker studied to become a qualified industrial training officer at the John Dalton College at Manchester Polytechnic. In 1972 he was appointed the first full-time Secretary of the newly constituted Nautical Institute. In 1982 he was elected a Fellow.

Since then Nautical Institute membership has expanded from 1,500 to over 6,000 and continues to grow internationally. The Institute's primary aim is to promote high standards of knowledge, competence and qualification amongst those in control of seagoing craft. The Institute's journal *Seaways* is recognised as the authoritative voice of the qualified mariner.

Mr Parker ran a regular feature in *Seaways* called Incident Desk which has now been superseded by the Confidential Marine Accident Reporting Scheme (MARS).

NAVIGATIONAL AND SEAMANSHIP INCIDENTS—COULD THEY HAVE BEEN AVOIDED?

PART I

GENERAL

NAVIGATION, in its broadest sense, has often been described as a science and an art. Whilst this was undoubtably true of the techniques and learning necessary to conquer the frontiers of the unknown, the same reasoning can not be applied to accident prevention for if it is a scientific activity, it should be possible to develop appropriate hypotheses and test them. If it is an art, it should be possible to carry out comparative studies and reach sensible conclusions. Neither approach, however, provides the full understanding of the subject.

The reasons are inherent in the methodology. For a scientific evaluation to be made the outcome must be repeatable. Few marine accidents fall into this category. If a comparative approach is to be used, then similar operating practices must be assumed and these can not be verified outside the confines of an organisation. When it comes to decision making there are a wide variety of individuals who influence performance standards and it is not possible to know what each person is thinking, either on board or ashore.

There are, however, data which research can provide, such as the number of incidents, their type and consequences; the frequency of accidents with respect to traffic density, flow or encounter rate; or commercial indicators in terms of cost. Inevitably the people collecting and interpreting the data are not the operators and this brings into focus another aspect of the issue which is communication.

The purpose of this paper is to ask whether there is a problem and if so what can be done about it. In doing so it is necessary to have an open mind. For nowhere is there a greater emotional tendency, particularly amongst professional navigators, to focus on one terrible incident and assume that all ships might be similarly operated. The derogatory remark like 'it's another flag of convenience ship' sums up this feeling. Yet the reality is that ships flying flags of convenience now make up nearly 70 per cent of the world fleet and on normal error rates they can be expected to have at least 70 per cent of the accidents.

The overview

The Institute of London Underwriters statistics probably provide the best indication of trends for total losses due to strandings and collisions worldwide and are recorded in figure 1:

However, the study carried out for the European Commission in 1987[2] revealed that the total loss rate provides an inadequate assessment of the number of incidents, their causes, or their risk factors. The COST 301 figures are dated and are currently being revised for another European study. They do, nonetheless, provide lines of enquiry which are essential to the understanding of risk at sea and how to manage it.

The study examined incidents between Suez and Murmansk and demonstrated that:

● Vessels of the world fleet will in the 1990s produce at least the same amount of ship miles as in 1982, caused by an improved ratio between sea time and port time.

This chart also includes the loss ratio (in percentage terms).

Nature of casualty	1988		1989		1990		1991		1992		average 1998-1992	
	No.	Gr. Tons	No.	Gr.Tons	No.	Gr. Tons	No.	Gr. Tons	No.	Gr. Tons	No.	Gr. Tons
Weather	44	309,340	52	293,330	51	551,666	64	637,976	27	371,819	48	430,000
Grounding	13	129,275	19	126,530	20	196,442	23	201,082	8	44,533	17	140,000
Collision/contact	7	41,529	21	71,571	14	95,181	18	72,033	17	210,772	15	98,000
Fire & explosion	20	250,768	28	211,831	31	289,655	36	513,929	21	196,184	27	292,000
Machinery, etc.	9	56,954	9	42,988	9	28,045	12	56,106	6	147,216	7	66,000
Miscellaneous or unknown	22	57,437	16	67,473	19	194,410	29	255,864	32	108,851	24	137,000
TOTALS	115	845,303	145	813,723	144	1,355,399	182	1,736,990	111	1,079,375	139	1,166,000
World tonnage		393,798,970		400,697,502		413,515,356		425,656,879		433,984,274		413,530,000
Loss ratio (%)		0 21		0.20		0.33		0.41		0.25		0.28

Fig. 1: World total losses 1988-92

- Collisions occur frequently in ports, but the number of collisions occuring at sea and in restricted waters is also high.

- Strandings occur mostly at sea. The number of strandings in restricted waters is far less.

- Thursday had the highest number of accidents, Tuesday the lowest.

- There are about 4,000 trading vessels at sea in European waters on any day, 600 of which are coastal vessels.

- Between 1978 and 1982 inclusive there were 119 meeting collisions, 66 crossing collisions and 26 overtaking collisions (excluding ports).

- There were 206 strandings in the same period (excluding ports).

- A trading vessel will become involved in a collision or a stranding on an average of 2,000,000 nautical miles travelled in European waters.

- In general, small and large vessels are more accident prone than vessels in the intermediate GT class.

- There was no significant difference in loss rates between EEC flag and non-EEC flag vessels.

When it comes to the cost of strandings and collisions, the situation is well documented by the insurance industry and the trends can be seen from the figures provided by the Institute of London

Estimated cost of total losses 1982-92

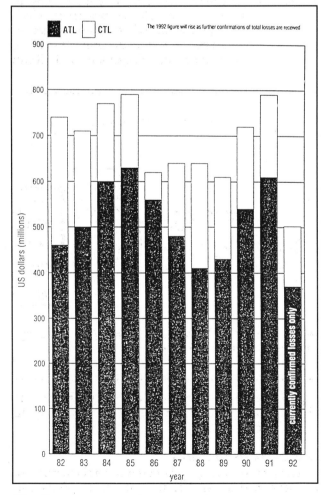

Fig. 2.

Underwriters[1] for the world fleet with respect to actual and constructive total losses (see figure 2).

It can be seen that whilst the numbers of incidents remain fairly constant and if anything are becoming fewer, the costs are increasing. This is because ships are larger and more sophisticated and reflects the increasing costs of repairs and compensation.

When the costs of claims are analysed by the insurance company or P&I Club there are two components—the actual payout of the claim and the administrative overhead in processing the claim. Premiums, therefore, have to cover these elements. Insurance companies are in competition with each other, but will seek to avoid processing uneconomic claims by raising the deductible. The Central Union of Marine Underwriters in Norway, for example, stated in their 1992 annual report: 'It appeared that claims with a final cost of less than $5,000 represented nearly 25 per cent of the number of claims processed'.

This means that many small incidents occur but will not be recorded in insurance companies, if their value is less than the deductible.

Costs of collisions and groundings to a shipping company

Insurance is paid for out of operating budgets and is divided into Hull & Machinery and P&I. Typically, a company will pay the following in premiums:

- 50,000 dwt Bulker   H&M $250,000 pa
- 50,000 dwt Bulker   P&I $120,000 pa

The trend from recent Press reports is to suggest that these figures will go up significantly in future. A further breakdown of costs by ship type can be obtained in the Drewry publication *Ship Costs: Their Structure and Significance.*[3]

From the point of view of this paper it must be observed that Hull & Machinery insurance typically covers all relevant risks but not all is related to navigation. Similarly, P&I insurance is for a range of cover which is not simply applied to collisions and strandings. The table (figure 3) from the UK Club puts this into perspective.[4]

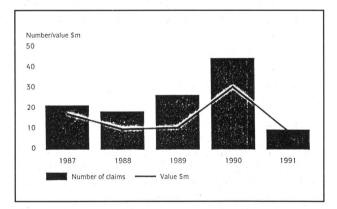

Fig. 3.

Costs of collisions and strandings to the industry

Assuming that collisions and strandings represent about one quarter of the causes of total losses for Hull & Machinery, then the overall cost per annum is about

$US200 million. Assuming that the UK Club underwrites one-fifth of the world fleet and its collision claims amount to $15m, the world fleet P&I cost will be about $75m. Applying the same logic to property damage (i.e., docks, wharfs, cranes, etc.) then the cost related to the world fleet is approximately $75m also. Excluding the consequential costs of pollution it can be seen that navigationally-related accidents are costing about $350 million per annum.

There are about 80,000 ships with an average of five deck officers each (taking into account leave, etc.). This makes a population of about 400,000 officers. If it is assumed that a one-week intensive course in navigational team work will reduce accidents by 25 per cent, then the pay-off between the cost of training and a saving of one quarter of $350 million can be evaluated—e.g., $88 million.

This works out at about $220 per officer, and begs the question whether it would be cost effective for the insurance industry to provide a training rebate of $250 for every officer who attends an approved navigational short course. The figures become even more attractive when it is realised that losses are occuring annually, but training may only need to be undertaken once every five years.

Certainly managers should seriously approach underwriters with this training argument—even if there is no rebate, it should be possible to demonstrate improvements in navigational safety for time spent training—a theme which is expanded in Section III relating to the human factor.

Consequential losses

Because the shipping industry maintains there is a low level of navigational accidents it has to be observed that the cost of insurance is unlikely to be a determining factor in implementing a change of policy. However, it is the consequential costs following an incident, which do not appear in the balance sheet, which need to be avoided.

For companies which have accidents the costs can be considerably more than the damages which are unlikely to be fully recovered. The costs are related to:

(i) Investigating the circumstances and visiting the ship.

(ii) The administrative time and cost of processing a claim.

(iii) The possible rescheduling/taking out of service of the vessel.

(iv) The redistribution of cargo.

(v) Organising the dry dock.

(vi) Organising a replacement vessel.

(vii) Organising redeployment of the crew.

For tanker companies, following a pollution incident, there will be additional costs associated with contingency planning, media response, pollution response and claims handling. There will also be penalties through public response and loss of market share for brand name distribution.

For the passenger ship companies, there is the added burden of abandoning a cruise, returning passengers to their destination, processing compensation, rescheduling the ship, acquiring stand-in tonnage and again loss of revenue through public response. Should an incident lead to litigation then the whole process will be extended with the Court hearing

becoming another major anxiety and costs to be overcome.

Costs to governments

It might be stated that the cost of administering a national Merchant Shipping Act is the accumulative cost of past accidents. Worldwide, The Nautical Institute estimates that this cost amounts to some $300 million annually.[5]

Following a major incident involving loss of life or marine pollution the costs to government can be exceedingly high and relate to:

(i) The casualty inquiry.

(ii) Political response.

(iii) Legislative response and consultation.

(iv) Human and emotional interest through media intervention and demands for response.

(v) Implementation of more costly accident avoidance measures.

(vi) Adverse influence on shipping for the flag State through higher costs.

(vii) Effort to influence international opinion.

One has to be continually reminded that it is society which finances and pays for shipping services. The finances may be provided by the pension funds used by investment banks. Similarly, it is the public who pay for transport in the costs of goods and services they buy. In so doing the public exerts a competitive pressure wanting to keep costs down, but following an incident it is the level of cultural awareness which determines their perception of acceptable practice. This is well illustrated in the diagram (figure 4) developed by Kasperson, Kasperson and Renn 1992:[6]

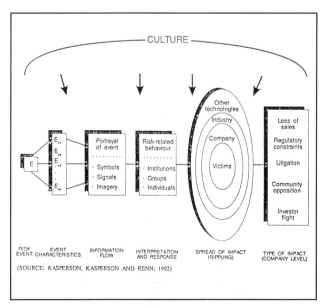

Fig. 4. Representation of social amplification of risk and its potential impacts on a risk managing organization.

Conclusion to Part I

The picture emerging from the general overview of accident analysis is that the rate of collisions and strandings are not increasing, but that the costs and damages are rising. The incidents of collisions are related to traffic density and vary with ship type.

A collision or stranding can be expected to occur at a frequency of 1 per 2 million nautical miles steamed.

The insurance costs to a company are unlikely to be the major contributory factor in changing company policy with respect to collisions and strandings. However, this is misleading evidence based upon past performance. The fact is that in a highly competitive industry where profit margins are very slim, the company assumes a much higher level of risk with respect to a major incident. Quite literally, it may not be able to afford the consequences. Shipping companies and governments share a common interest in seeking to avoid consequential losses following an incident.

Upgrading the quality of navigational team work is likely to be cost effective.

The level of 'acceptable risk' varies from country to country. Where there is a well developed mass media distribution system, it is likely that the impact of a shipping disaster will be magnified. The social response will inevitably be to overreact to avoid a similar incident, thereby compounding the cost to society. It would be sensible for the shipping industry to develop strategies to reduce the number of accidents.

PART II

STRANDINGS AND COLLISIONS

STRANDINGS

1. El Paso Paul Kayser

Captain Oddvan Bangsund was the competent, well-trained and experienced master of *El Paso Paul Kayser*. He had loaded LNG at Arzew, Algeria, and was heading for Cove Point, Maryland, through the Strait of Gibraltar. As he was approaching the strait on a course of 274° true, he missed his intended alter-course position when 9.4 miles from Europa Point, Gibraltar (see figure 5). On prior voyages it was at that point that he would head 252° true to enter the traffic separation scheme.

Captain Bangsund delayed altering course when faced with crossing incoming traffic headed north. He again missed an opportunity to turn southwest owing to an approaching cross-channel passenger/car ferry coming out of Gibraltar Bay from Algeciras. He forfeited his last opportunity to head safely south when a fishing boat crossed his bow. When the master finally ordered hard to port, he was less than a mile off the Spanish coast. He placed *El Paso Paul Kayser* astride a granite pinnacle.

The Liberian enquiry[6] stated that the reason for the incident was 'the failure to have, and execute, a written passage plan'. The report also demonstrated that the collision avoidance system (CAS) was being used and the master placed more reliance on the CAS than on his experienced seaman's eye. Lack of bridge organisation inhibited the awareness which checks would have provided.

Comment

The case has special interest in that the presentation of ARPAs can appear so comprehensive with respect to other ships in the vicinity that situational awareness can be lost.

2. Exxon Valdez

'After the pilot ladder was secured, the AB assisting the third mate returned to his lookout station on the bow. The third mate then returned to the bridge, arriving there between 2334 and 2336. According to the third mate, the vessel was on course 200° when he arrived on the bridge and he believed the engine was speeding up to 55 rpm (about 11 knots) to match the order for full-ahead manoeuvring speed. The bell book indicates that the vessel was placed on 'load program up' at 2352 (the speed of the main engine was being increased slowly by a computer from manoeuvring full ahead (55 rpm) to full-ahead sea speed (78.9 rpm), requiring about 43 minutes). The third mate stated that the master, before leaving the bridge, placed the vessel on load program up (see figure 6).

'Shortly after the third mate returned to the bridge, the master informed the third mate that he (the master) would be bringing the vessel to 180° to avoid ice, and the master directed the third mate to take a fix of the vessel's position. The course recorder trace showed that the course change was started about 2339. The third mate took a visual bearing of Busby Island Light and Buoy No. 9 and a radar range to the land

Fig. 5. Stranding—LNG carrier El Paso Paul Kayser—29 June 1979

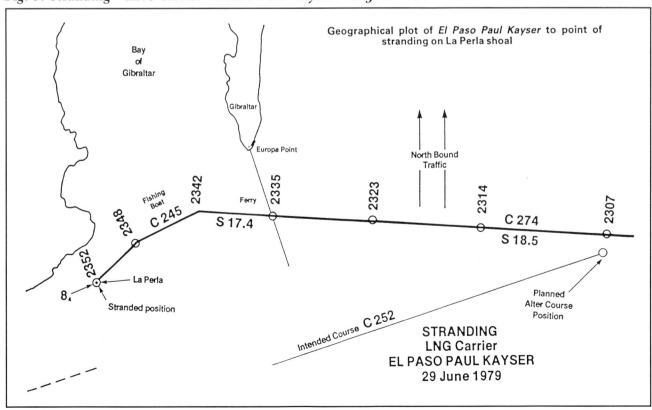

adjacent to Buoy No. 9. The third mate stated that the vessel was turning while he was taking the bearings. When plotted, his fix showed that the vessel's 2339 position was in the middle of the separation zone and approximately 2 miles west of Rocky Point Light. By about 2343, according to the course recorder, the vessel was steady on a course of 180°.

'The third mate testified that he had determined by radar that there was a distance of about 0.9 mile between Bligh Reef and the ice floe and that it would be possible to pass around the ice once Busby Island Light was abeam. The master left the bridge about 2352. The third mate testified that he thought it would not be possible to turn sooner because of the ice. The third mate also testified that he never considered slowing the vessel because the decision had been made to avoid the ice rather than to proceed through it.

'The third mate claimed that because he expected to change course in a few minutes, he went to the steering stand and pushed the hand steering button, removing the vessel from automatic pilot and placing it in hand steering. According to the third mate, the helmsman also attempted to push the hand steering button. He testified that he observed the indicator on the consol illuminate, signifiying that the steering system was in hand steering mode.

'The third mate observed Busby Island on the radar and determined that the vessel would be about 0.9 mile from Busby Island Light when the light became abeam to port. The third mate then walked to the port wing of the bridge and took a visual bearing of Busby Island Light when it was abeam. At that time, while still on the wing of the bridge, he observed that the time on his watch was 2355. He then proceeded to the chart room, located in the after port side of the wheelhouse, to plot the fix. Although the third mate stated that the vessel was about 0.9 mile from Busby Island Light, he plotted the 2355 position 1.1 mile from the light.

'The third mate claimed that shortly after he plotted the 2355 fix, he ordered the helmsman to put the rudder to right 10°. He estimated that he issued the order for right 10° rudder about a minute after taking the visual bearing on the port bridge wing. He did not recall watching the rudder angle indicator to ensure that the rudder was actually applied.

'About this time, the lookout again entered the wheelhouse to report that the red light on the starboard bow was flashing every 4 seconds instead of 5 seconds. She found the third mate at the port radar, and he again acknowledged her report in a calm, routine manner. At this time, according to the third mate, he looked out, sighted the light, and identified it as Bligh Reef buoy. The lookout returned to the starboard wing of the bridge, and a short time later, she noticed that the vessel was beginning to swing slowly to the right.

'According to the third mate, the radar indicated that the ship was still following a 180° track, although the vessel's heading was swinging right. The third mate then ordered hard right rudder. He estimated that Bligh Reef buoy was about 2 points (22½°) on the port bow by this time that about 2 minutes had elapsed from the time of his order for right 20° rudder until he ordered hard right rudder.

'After several seconds at the radar, following the order for hard right rudder, the third mate telephoned the master and said, "I think we are in serious trouble".'

Comment

This brief extract from the comprehensive report prepared by the US National Transportation Board deserves careful analysis. The reason for the misjudgement of the third mate was given as *the third mate's failure to turn the vessel at the proper time and with sufficient rudder was the result of his excessive work load and fatigued condition, which caused him to lose awareness of the location of Bligh Reef.*

The crucial point of this brief extract is that the third mate was undoubtedly practising what he had been taught. More significantly, it is quite possible to envisage a similar scenario in another location where the same loss of situational awareness could occur, because the officer was applying the general practice of merchant marine navigation.

3. Sundancer

During the forenoon of 29 June, 1984 the *Sundancer* arrived at Ballantyne Pier, Vancouver, British Columbia, Canada. Upon arrival, passengers from the second cruise disembarked and shortly afterwards passengers for the third cruise commenced embarking. New passengers continued to join the vessel during the afternoon and at the same time 13 vehicles belonging to some of the passengers were driven on board.

Two Pacific Coast pilots boarded the vessel at about 1630 hours. At 1715 hours, 29 June, 1984, the *Sundancer* sailed from Ballantyne Pier, Vancouver, with 292 crew members, 495 passenger and 13 vehicles, bound for Juneau, Alaska, the first port of call of a seven-day cruise. Shortly after departure from Ballantyne Pier, the passengers were assembled at their lifeboat stations to be instructed in the method of wearing their lifejackets and where to assemble in case an emergency should arise.

The passage northward through the Strait of Georgia was normal and uneventful. At 2158 hours on 29 June, 1984 the *Sundancer* passed Cape Lazo and shortly afterwards overtook the cruise vessel *Daphne*. This had been pre-arranged by the pilots on board the respective vessels. The *Sundancer* reported at 2303 hours by VHF radio telephone to Vessel Traffic Services that she was passing Cape Mudge, which is located on Quadra Island at the southern entrance to Discovery Passage. The vessel continued northward through Discovery Passage, passing Steep Island at 2330 hours, reporting at that time to VTS that they expected to be at Separation Head at about 2350 hours. Separation Head is located on the northern side of Seymour Narrows.

As the vessel passed Race Point, an alteration of course was made to steer for the green light located at Wilfred Point on the western side of Seymour Narrows. The vessel steadied on a course with the green light slightly on the starboard bow. As she approached closer to Maud Island it became apparent that the vessel was rapidly closing in to the rocky beach. Numerous helm and engine movements were

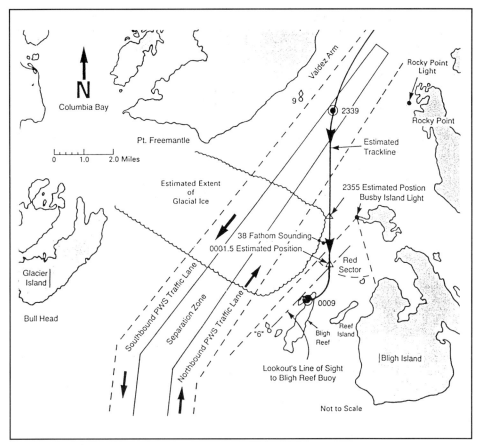

Fig. 6 Trackline of Exxon Valdez

given in an attempt to prevent the vessel from running aground. The execution of these movements was too late; consequently the vessel struck bottom as she was swinging to port away from the rugged shoreline.

The time of striking bottom was recorded at 2356 hours 29 June 1984, the weather being fine and clear. After striking bottom, she continued her forward progress but as it became apparent that the damge required assessment, the vessel manoeuvred slowly into Menzies Bay. During this time the vessel developed a list of about 5° to starboard due to ingress of water through damaged double bottoms and shell plating.

As the *Sundancer* approached a suitable anchoring position in Menzies Bay it became evident that there were two tugs together with assist boats towing two log booms in the vicinity. The *Sundancer* eventually anchored in Menzies Bay at approximately 0010 hours, 30 June 1984.

Comment

The Canadian accident investigation board stated[8] that the stranding occurred because:

> *Those in charge of the navigation of the vessel failed to ensure that the correct course was being steered to clear Maud Island . . . the necessary action to counteract the strong ebb current . . . was not taken; . . . the navigation of the vessel was not conducted from the centre line of the ship in the wheelhouse and, due to the short forecastle hampering perspective, the apparent course could not be fully appreciated.*

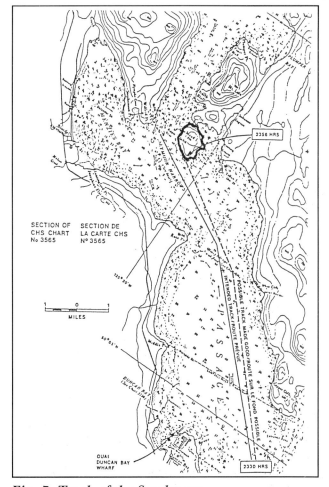

Fig. 7. Track of the Sundancer

The incident is particularly interesting and is one used in The Nautical Institute Command Diploma Scheme as a case study. The ship had two pilots on board, but the passage was so critical that in all probability there would not have been time to alert the pilot to the fact that the vessel was deviating from the plan following a position fix. From the evidence in the report it appears that the pilot was navigating by using his relative sense keeping Maud Island light ahead. Why else would he have ordered starboard wheel when the vessel was already to the right of track?

The case is invaluable as a training exercise for masters, because they have to be able to answer the question 'How could you have prevented the accident from occurring?'.

There is one universal point which affects navigation and collision avoidance and that is the misuse of relative bearings. The effect is only felt in areas with strong cross currents or where wind causes significant leeway. Similarly, only certain types of manoeuvre demonstrate a change in relative bearing when in fact the approaching vessel is on a changing collision course (see figure 8).

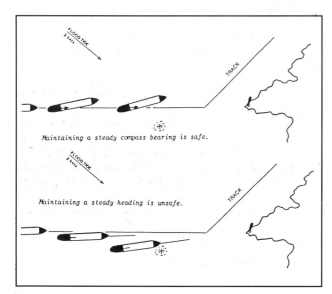

Fig. 8

The need to take compass bearings or bearings from the radar can be illustrated in the two diagrams. In Fig. 9 the relative and true bearings are coincidentally similar. In Fig. 10 it is the compass bearing which is constant and indicates risk of collision.

To introduce any discussion on pilotage all students must be asked if they would be tempted to use relative bearings. The pitfalls need to be explained. This might appear to be an unwarranted attention to a particular detail, but it lies at the culture of merchant marine navigation to fix the ship and compensate between fixes for any set and drift. Pilotage techniques of using compass bearings or compass related parallel index are still generally not practised, which means that on most ships a pilot error could easily go undetected.

Conclusions to the strandings section

The three cases used to illustrate this part of the paper are very unlikely to happen to the same

individuals, but could easily happen again elsewhere.

The significance of relative and compass bearings must be fully appreciated.

It is always asssumed that managers and super-intendents know what is expected from their fleet in terms of navigational performance; but, with so much interchange at sea today, is it realistic to assume a common standard?

Collisions

1. European Gateway/Speedlink Vanguard

At about 2251 on the night of 19 December 1982, the *European Gateway* collided in clear visibility with the *Speedlink Vanguard* in the approaches to the port of Harwich. The *European Gateway*, holed on the starboard side, immediately began to list to starboard. She flooded and within ten minutes of the collision was lying on her starboard side, having grounded with her port side clear of the water. Most of those on the *European Gateway* were taken off the ship, after she capsized, by rescue vessels. A number of men, however, jumped or were thrown into the sea. Of these, two passengers and four crew members lost their lives.

The collision occurred outside and to the north of that section of the dredged channel which is marked by buoys No. 3 and No. 5. The *Speedlink Vanguard* was inward bound to the Harwich Train Terminal at Parkeston Quay and the *European Gateway* was outward bound from Felixstowe. Prior to the collision, the *Speedlink Vanguard* had been navigating within

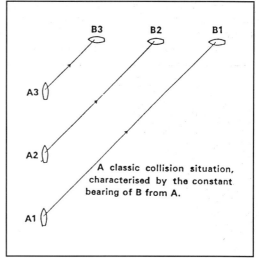

Fig 9

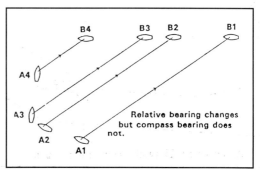

Fig. 10

the dredged channel, though close to the northern edge (see figure 11).

Captain H. H. McGibney, who was in charge of the navigation of the *European Gateway*, had intended to cross ahead of the *Speedlink Vanguard* before the *Speedlink Vanguard* reached Cork Spit and then to alter course to starboard to proceed on an easterly course outside the dredged channel, passing the *Speedlink Vanguard* starboard to starboard. He thought that he could rely upon the *Speedlink Vanguard* to remain in the dredged channel.

Captain J. Bolton, who was in charge of the navigation of the *Speedlink Vanguard*, expected the *European Gateway* to round to starboard at Cork Spit and to pass his vessel port to port in the dredged channel. He altered course to starboard to give the *European Gateway* more room for the turn and, subsequently, put his wheel hard to starboard in an attempt to avoid collision. In fact, this action brought the *Speedlink Vanguard* into collision with the *European Gateway*, which had stood on out of the channel to the north without significant alteration of course or speed.

The collision would not have occurred had not Captain Bolton mistaken the intentions of the *European Gateway*. Much of the investigation centred on the question of who was responsible for the confusion that developed. As was to be expected those representing the vessels and their masters adopted adversarial positions.

The *Speedlink Vanguard* initially struck the *European Gateway* just forward of amidships, but the main impact was into the *European Gateway* in way of the generator room. The *European Gateway* was breached at two levels. The bow visor of the *Speedlink Vanguard* tore open the *European Gateway*'s shell plating at main and upper deck level. The bulbous bow smashed into the generator room, driving in a distance of some 2 metres from the side shell.

The inquiry[9] made only one navigational recommendation following this incident: 'The UK Department of Transport should recognise that modern radar provides an alternative to compass bearings as a means of detecting risk of collision and, in future, M Notices on this topic should emphasise the importance of proper use of radar for this purpose'.

Comment

Professional opinion is divided as to who might most have been at fault in this case. It was a situation also in a VTS area when there was misunderstanding and an accident occurred. The practical response to this casualty was to separate inbound and outbound traffic through the use of separation schemes.

2. Confidential Accident Report Near Miss(es) No. 92008

MARS 92008. Two near misses in Port Approaches Night time. Visibility:— 0500—2 miles. 0520—1 mile. 0540—0.6 miles. 0660—0.3 miles.

Vessels involved (See figure 12):
A Medium size tanker in ballast, at anchor.
B Car carrier, disembarks pilot at 0530.
C Coaster, no pilot, looking for anchorage.
D Medium size tanker in ballast, disembarks pilot at 0535.
E Large car carrier, pilot disembarks 0537, not monitoring VHF Ch. 16 or VTS Channel. Set course parallel to and on starboard quarter of **D**.
F Large loaded ore carrier, restricted entry time due to draught, pilot on board, not making way, waiting for **D** and **E** to clear.

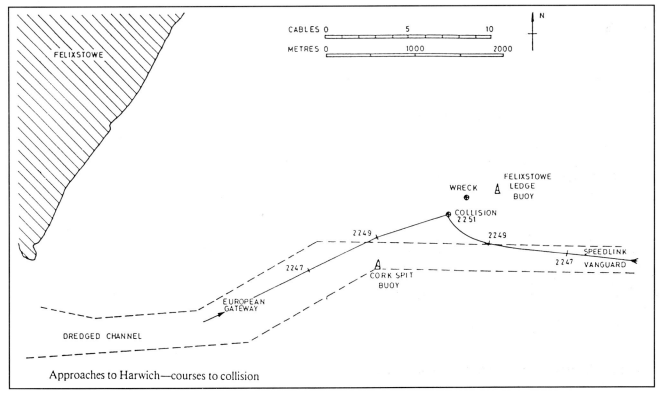

Approaches to Harwich—courses to collision

Fig. 11

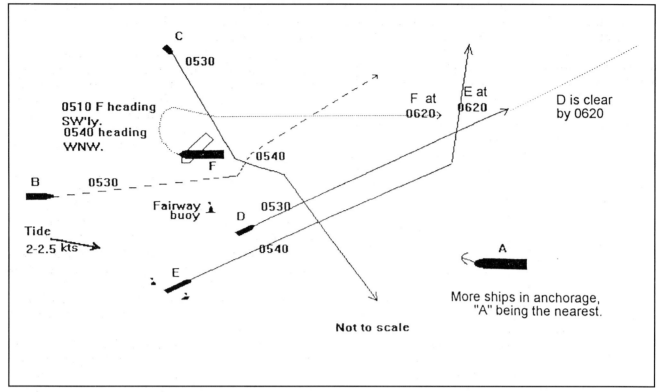

Fig. 12

Events:—

D clears port and steams away.
B heads for gap between **D** and **F**.
F loses sight of **C** as visibility decreases.
C heads to pass astern of **F**.

C talks to **B** on VTS working channel. Radar echo of **B** is probably obscured aboard **C** by **F**, and **C** assumes that **E** is **B**. The only vessel not communicating on VHF is **E**. A close encounter occurs between **B** and **C**. Both go hard-a-port, and narrowly avoid a collision. **F** swings slowly to starboard away from shallow water to seek anchorage. **E** gradually increases speed and suddenly alters course 70 degrees to port. **F** eventually finds **E** on VHF Channel 9, **E** assures **F** that everything is all right and proceeds pass 2.5 cables ahead of **F** at 14 knots in 3 cables visibility.

Causes: Congestion, lack of discipline, assumption, Port radar non-operational.

3. Nordpol and HMCS Kootenay

On 1 June, at about 0400, HMCS *Kootenay* began an anti-submarine exercise in a 3 square mile assigned area just north of practice zone W601. The existence of this temporary zone, which is not marked on the chart, was known only to the Armed Forces. The operation was a simulation of wartime conditions and the surface ship's task was to identify the hull of the submersible vessel.

To reduce the eventuality of detection by the submarine, HMCS *Kootenay* was operating in a passive sense; the emission of electromagnetic waves was at as low a level as possible, the operational radars were restricted, but a sophisticated electronic sensing device was in use. A continuous listening radio watch was maintained on VHF Channels 16 and 74 and no communication was established with Tofino VTS Centre before the collision.

Because of the reduced visibility due to thick fog, in addition to the two lookouts posted, one on each bridge wing, a lookout was posted on the bow as well as a 'lifebuoy' sentry on the stern of the vessel. Data acquired from the on-board electronic sensing device concerning the presence of the *Nordpol* was not relayed to the bridge and the sole means of detecting her available to the bridge personnel was by aural and visual lookout.

In the last 20 minutes before the impact, HMCS *Kootenay*, in attempting to find the submarine had, for tactical reasons, frequently altered her course and speed; courses had been altered at intervals not exceeding 6 minutes and the speed of the vessel had been increased from 5 knots to 6.7 knots.

The presence of the *Nordpol* was first detected by the forward lookout who heard the sound of her bow wave, and the information was transmitted vocally and by manual indication of its direction, to the bridge. A few seconds later, visual contact was established by the OOW on the bridge; the *Nordpol* bore a relative bearing of red 20°. The two main engines were immediately ordered full speed astern. No steering orders were given. The commanding officer, who was in the operations room, rushed to the bridge.

At 0726, HMCS *Kootenay* collided with the *Nordpol*.

At 1805 on 31 May, 1989, the *Nordpol* departed Vancouver bound for Singapore with a load of 49,968 tonnes of sulphur and 10,253 tonnes of potash. At 0042 on 1 June, the pilot disembarked off Victoria and the vessel proceeded down Juan de Fuca Strait. At 0115, Race Rocks light was rounded and fog was observed to roll in from the sea. A lookout was posted on the bridge and the master remained in the wheelhouse.

On exiting Seattle Traffic Zone at 0514, the *Nordpol* passed abeam meridian 124° 40'W and reported a course of 290° (G) at 13.5 knots to Tofino Traffic Centre. She was advised of the traffic ahead and warned about fishing activity along her course line. At 0530, a radar fix was taken aboard the vessel and the course was altered to 270° (G).

At 0542, the *Nordpol* requested information on several unidentified targets 2.5 miles ahead. No activity was observed by the Tofino VTS Centre at that distance, but the marine traffic regulator informed the *Nordpol*, about the presence of targets approximately 4 miles away which, presumably, were fishing vessels. The radars were monitored by the master and chief officer but no vessel was detected and the targets were presumed to be sea clutter. A few minutes later, amongst the ten or so targets on the radar screen, one target at a 10-12 miles distance near the heading marker caught the chief officer's attention. As with all other targets it was manually acquired and tracked by the ARPA radar repeater.

Between 0712-0714, the *Nordpol* switched to VHF Channel 16 and tried unsuccessfully to establish radio contact with the unidentified vessel ahead of her. The vessel *Stardancer*, taking part in a radio conversation involving a close-quarters situation, was momentarily mistaken for the unidentified vessel. However, as the conversation developed, the *Nordpol* realised it did not concern her.

A continuous plot on the 3-cm radar revealed that the target was moving in a northerly direction and then parallel to the heading marker in a generally easterly direction. The chief officer assumed the target to be a fishing vessel and the *Nordpol* stood on with her speed and course.

Subsequently, the target adopted a southeasterly direction about 1 mile away. The 3-cm radar range was reduced down to 3 miles and the cursor was aligned with the target. To confirm his observation, the chief officer once again monitored the ARPA repeater until the target came within 0.5 mile distance, at which time the master was called and informed that risk of collision existed.

Back at the 3-cm radar, the target was observed for a moment to take a course to pass astern of the *Nordpol*, then directly towards the vessel. At 0725, the main engine was stopped and a warship was observed coming out of the fog one point on the starboard bow.

At 0726, the *Nordpol* and HMCS *Kootenay* were involved in a collision in a position determined by *Nordpol* to be 48° 30.7'N and 125° 24.9'W. The *Nordpol* was proceeding at full economic speed on a course of 268° (G). Reportedly the impact occurred at approximately right angles.

The inquiry analysed the incident through the implementation of the International Regulations for Preventing Collisions at Sea, under the headings: Application, Rule 1; Responsibility, Rule 2; Lookout, Rule 5; Safe Speed, Rule 6; Risk of Collision, Rule 7; Action to avoid Collision, Rule 8; Conduct of vessels in Restricted Visibility, Rule 19; Application, Rule 20; Power-driven vessels under way, Rule 23; Sound Signals, Rule 35.

RECONSTRUCTION OF THE TRACKS OF THE "KOOTENAY" AND THE "NORDPOL"

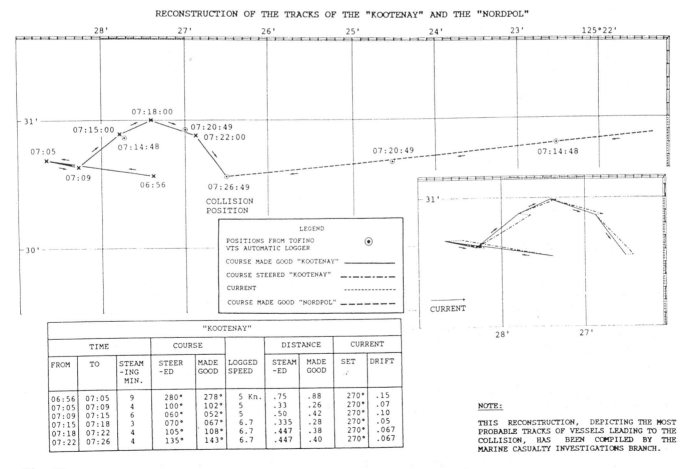

LEGEND

POSITIONS FROM TOFINO VTS AUTOMATIC LOGGER	⊙
COURSE MADE GOOD "KOOTENAY"	———
COURSE STEERED "KOOTENAY"	—·—·—·—
CURRENT	- - - - - - -
COURSE MADE GOOD "NORDPOL"	— — — — —

"KOOTENAY"									
TIME			COURSE			DISTANCE		CURRENT	
FROM	TO	STEAM-ING MIN.	STEER-ED	MADE GOOD	LOGGED SPEED	STEAM-ED	MADE GOOD	SET	DRIFT
06:56	07:05	9	280°	278°	5 Kn.	.75	.88	270°	.15
07:05	07:09	4	100°	102°	5	.33	.26	270°	.07
07:09	07:15	6	060°	052°	5	.50	.42	270°	.10
07:15	07:18	3	070°	067°	6.7	.335	.28	270°	.05
07:18	07:22	4	105°	108°	6.7	.447	.38	270°	.067
07:22	07:26	4	135°	143°	6.7	.447	.40	270°	.067

NOTE:

THIS RECONSTRUCTION, DEPICTING THE MOST PROBABLE TRACKS OF VESSELS LEADING TO THE COLLISION, HAS BEEN COMPILED BY THE MARINE CASUALTY INVESTIGATIONS BRANCH.

Fig. 13

Comment

The case was chosen because, although rare, collisions between warships and merchant vessels do occur. Unlike fishing vessels, warships on exercise can not exempt themselves from complying with the rules. Also the incident occurred within a VTS and the report stated:

Participation in the VTS was voluntary and when HMCS Kootenay proceeded beyond the Tofino VTS radar range the alpha-numeric identification tag was automatically lost and hence not retrieved as the ship re-entered the zone. Tofino VTS Centre assumed the target to be a fishing vessel since no relevant information other than the acknowledgement of its presence could be ascertained.

Again in this case we notice the use of VHF to try and establish identity and intention. Did this detract from taking early evasive action?

Conclusions to the collisions section

Shipping presents circumstances which are not always predictable. Collision situations generally involve both a knowledge of the Rules and experienced judgement in their application.

Watchkeeping officers need experience. Knowing when to call for assistance requires an understanding of how situations might develop and a well-rehearsed response when, say, the master comes to the bridge.

PART III

THE HUMAN ELEMENT

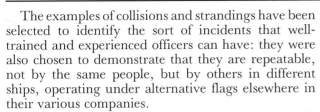

The examples of collisions and strandings have been selected to identify the sort of incidents that well-trained and experienced officers can have: they were also chosen to demonstrate that they are repeatable, not by the same people, but by others in different ships, operating under alternative flags elsewhere in their various companies.

There is another group of accidents caused by negligence and bad management which include groundings due to uncorrected charts and watch-keepers leaving the bridge for a variety of reasons during their watch.

It has been stated since records were first collected that most (typically 75-80 per cent) of all collisions and strandings are caused by human error. This statistic only has meaning if we know the number of incidents involved. As was shown in Part I, human element related incidents are not increasing in number.

What then should be the aim? To reduce the percentage of human errors from, say, 75 per cent to 50 per cent or to reduce the total number of accidents by 20 per cent? Clearly the two aims are related, but to identify the specific areas where success is most likely to be found it is necessary to analyse causes and effects with a view to focusing limited resources to achieve the best results.

Governmental analysis

The study initiated by the German Government and reported by the Institute of Shipping Economics and Logistics in Bremen during the period 1987-91 revealed that, with respect to German ships, failure to comply with the International Regulations for Preventing Collisions at Sea accounted for the highest proportion of incidents at 23.1 per cent. The breakdown of human failures is given in the following table[12].

Failure to observe the ColRegs	23.1%
Navigation faults	20.5%
Failure to comply with safety regulations	14.1%
Inadequate watchkeeping	11.3%
Other human failures	12.4%
Bad seamanship	11.1%
Faulty handling of equipment	7.5%

The UK Government commissioned the Tavistock Institute to analyse *The Human Element in Shipping Casualties*[13]. The report reveals much valuable information contained in the government's investigators' records.

Collisions

'The pilot study estimated that human error was involved in 96 per cent of collisions . . . in none of the cases looked at was one ship wholly to blame. Among a total of 39 cases the following items were identified:

Carelessness and overconfidence	7
Lack of attention	6
Errors of judgement	5
Communication failures	5
Lack of knowledge	3
Excessive speed in poor visibility	3

Sheer/interaction between ships	2
Steering failure	2
Incidents peculiar to special situations	6
One third occurred between 0300 and 0700	

Groundings

Sixteen causes of groundings and strandings were studied in depth. The following were identified in order of significance:

● General overconfidence to perceive hazards.

● Neglect to use the depth recorder.

● Errors in position fixing.

● Accidents tend to occur when approaching port rather than leaving port.

● Generally only one man was on the bridge when the grounding occurred.

● Poor planning.

● Most of the vessels were in the short-sea trades.

● Poor visibility was not as significant as for collisions.

● Very little supporting evidence of work patterns or watch systems aboard could be located in the records. It was therefore not possible to evaluate the effect of fatigue.

The report published by the UK P&I Club in their Analysis of Claims 1992 adds further detail in a global context:

Human error was the main cause of half the cargo claims, half the pollution claims, 65 per cent of personal injuries; 80 per cent of property damage and 90 per cent of collisions.

Collisions

Of the 123 claims, 82 per cent of the cases involved ships under way, whilst 20 per cent of those were under way at 'excessive speed'. The tables show the status of the ship and place of occurrence:

Status

Underway	62%
Underway at excessive speed	20%
At anchorage	9%
Berthing	6%
Others	3%

Place

Coastal waters	31%
Open water	22%
Separation zone	14%
In harbour	14%
River/canal	11%
At anchorage	7%
Other	1%

Type of collision

Crossing	39%
End on	25%
One ship static	20%
Overtaking	10%
Other	6%

The UK Club report also records that in 18 per cent of the incidents pilot error was identified as a significant factor and 32 per cent of the incidents occurred between 0400 and 0800. The master was on the bridge in 16 out of 21 collisions. It is also interesting to note that 62 per cent of collisions occurred in good or fair visibility and 76 per cent in slight seas.

Property damage

Very high levels of damage can occur in port areas and the UK Club report studied 156 claims and demonstrated that the main causes were as follows:

Pilot error	36%
Officer error	31%
Shore error	10%
Mechanical failure	10%
Crew error	6%
Equipment failure	3%
Structural failure	2%
Under investigation	2%

The report adds a number of observations which demonstrate that accidents in port areas also occur through other causes outside the control of the ship-owner. These include inappropriate berth design; the tugs ordered by the agent without consultation with the ship and, in cases where masters are paid if they avoid using tugs and pilots, commercial pressure can outweigh prudence.

Increasingly automated bridge equipment means that pilots and masters end up steering and manoeuvring the ships themselves; so restricting their movement on the bridge. Masters operating variable-pitch propellers 'superimpose their own input on to pilots' advice'.

Communications pose problems, particularly during pilotage phases and the report points out that there is no standard method of training pilots and this is a subject which the report concludes needs further study and improvement.

What executive action is needed?

It now becomes evident that the situation is confused by a variety of different management signals. Should the aim now be to reduce financial loss resulting from incidents or simply to reduce their frequency? If contact damage is significant, then should not pilots be brought into the discussion?

There are further ways of approaching accident statistics and these can be considered in terms of risk, knowledge and ignorance, mistakes and errors, behaviour and motivation. In each of these areas there can be a variety of perceptions, making it difficult to be sure just where to direct improvements. People are different, training varies, confidence beguiles, profit and risk go together.

Education and training

Whereas in the past it could be assumed that all officers on board had received similar training, the mixed manning policies of the last 15 years means that there will be wide variations in detailed education, quality of teaching, seatime, experience and company support for fleet standards.

Taking the IMO model course objectives for navigation (Annex 1) it becomes evident that they are directed towards giving *the individual* the knowledge and skills to navigate and take a watch. Mistakes and errors are, however, made by individuals and can only be overcome through an organisation which checks and verifies.

This part of navigation is not included in the curriculum, probably for the simple reason that it was thought to be unnecessary and that this operational activity would be picked up on board.

To give some idea of the wide variation in approaches to navigational training, it can be seen from the study conducted by Dr M. A. Aziz[14] that the proportion of time spent on each discipline varies according to country.

Mistakes and errors

If errors of ignorance can be avoided through education and training, what can be done to ensure that those already in the system fully understand the weaknesses in navigational management or their lack of up to date knowledge of the International Regulations for Preventing Collisions at Sea and how to interpret the Rules? There are two types of problem: those officers who believe that vessels in a traffic separation scheme have right of way over crossing vessels; and officers who know the Rules, but apply their experience, rather than the strict interpretation of the Rules—e.g., Rule 19.

In this latter respect, a study conducted by Captain Syms[15] demonstrated that over 80 per cent of officers, when asked to differentiate between action in clear weather and action in restricted visibility, got the answer wrong. It led Captain Syms to observe:

At this very moment, somewhere in the world, possibly in the crowded approach channels to one of the major world economic centres, two very large laden tankers, despite being in the same separation lane, are approaching each other in zero visibility from a broad angle, somewhat ambiguous direction. We now know there is a better than 80 per cent chance that the bridge personnel of both vessels will have a totally confused idea of the conduct required of them in this situation.

Where navigation is concerned, accidents have been caused by just about every kind of omission imaginable. A useful and salutary book dealing with strandings and their causes written by Captain R. A. Cahill concludes:

It is the disciplined approach to navigation as opposed to the haphazard that is advocated and that leaves ample scope for initiative.
In over half the cases studied the seamen involved came to grief not because they were lacking in skill and experience but because they relied too much on those attributes and failed to look ahead and attempt to foresee the difficulties that would develop and so take measures to deal with them.

In this brief discussion concerning mistakes and errors, it becomes almost impossible to train for every eventuality and it leads towards the idea of training in error avoidance as a conceptual idea.

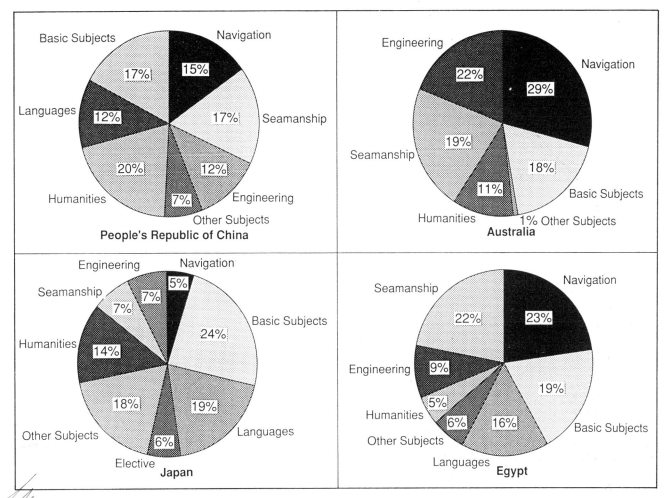

People's Republic of China

Australia

Japan

Egypt

Behaviour and motivation

People in authority behave differently from those in subordinate roles. If the whole culture of industrial training has been to respect those in authority and never question them, then an error made by a master or a pilot is likely to continue uncorrected by junior officers.

Dr David Moreby[16] in his study into multi-national manning pointed out that races, cultures and creeds carry with them specific expectations about behaviour which can work well in certain combinations but badly in others. He also observed:

The fact that officers from developing countries, will fill technical managerial positions ashore is neither good nor bad—it is simply economically sensible to have, in the owner's head office, technical managers (deck, engine and personnel superintendents) who share common values and language with the senior officers in the ships. So, another scenario for the future may be ships manned totally by foreign seafarers, plus technical managers in the company's head office drawn from the country of the seafarers—e.g., Indian superintendents ashore managing Indian-manned ships; or Filipino superintendents ashore managing Filipino-manned ships.

*Thus, to achieve commercial efficiency in cross-culturally-manned merchant ships, the owner must be able to communicate shared values **either** through a fellow national supercargo aboard his ship or through superintendents in his head office from the same country and culture as his crews.*

Motivation and morale are key factors in any human activity. Lethargy and boredom which result from a lack of interest are just as likely to lead to errors and omissions as overwork, tiredness and fatigue. It is also well known that the mind, like physical fitness, works more efficiently the more it is used and that after long periods of relatively low activity, it takes time to respond rapidly to situations of high activity.

In the *Nautical Briefing* on *Bridge Watchkeeping*[17] the Council of The Nautical Institute commented upon the subject of motivation by stating:

Motivation is not only difficult to define but depends upon personality, conditions, communications and rewards. It is necessary to be realistic in what can be achieved in a given situation. However, some general guidance can be given. In the first instance, it is the company's management which is responsible for creating the conditions which will encourage motivation in seagoing personnel. The master is then able to apply his energy to this all important aspect of ship management without having to resort to apologetic compromise.

Secondly, it is always easier to motivate people by involving them when planning ahead rather than only complaining if jobs have not been done properly.

Human nature defies detailed analysis and there is a perverse relationship between risk and routine. When individuals know they are taking risks their sense of excitement is increased and they become more alert.

When all operations have been reduced to boring monotonous procedures, there is clear evidence from numerous studies that the mind can wander and the unexpected can go unnoticed. Whilst these human attributes are well known, it is difficult to develop a consistent safety regime based upon fickle human nature.

This type of realisation has led Professor T. J. Reason[18] to develop a new approach to safety in which he describes the error causing influences as pathogens, always present and needing to be subdued. He stated:

> *Effective safety management (and hence the systems overall error tolerance) can only be achieved on the basis of relevant up-to-date information regarding the intrinsic safety state of the organisation. In short, safety managers need to take regular samplings of the organisation's vital signs of proactive safety state indicators.*

With the background of this paper, it is possible to identify company operations which deliver consistently good results:

Activity	Relevant factors
Recruitment	Assessment of capability and temperament.
Education	Examined to a proven standard.
Training (on board)	Planned to provide verified experience, and judgement.
Navigation policy	Clearly stated by company instructions and masters' standing orders, specified.
Job description	Clearly stated responsibilities.
Discipline	Specify in writing the conditions for: (i) Instant dismissal for gross navigational misconduct; (ii) Severe reprimand for negligence; (iii) Formal warnings for unacceptable practices.
Placement	Careful selection of bridge teams.
Operational learning	Passages planned—situations evaluated and discussed; drills practised, contingencies made; de-briefing after complex operations.
Inspection	Periodic inspection by competent company superintendent to ensure navigational standards are maintained.
Review (appraisal)	A recognised system for identifying specific training needs.
Cultural compatibility	Culturally in tune with officers and crew—crews themselves culturally compatible.
Awards	Support for good performance.

Relationships with outside organisations:

Discuss local navigational problems with pilots and port authorities
Keep Hydrographer informed of changes
Keep Government informed of incidents
Keep Nautical Institute informed of near misses.

Feedback

(i) Investigate incidents; inform fleet through circulars

(ii) Inform industry through Nautical Institute and other channels about near misses and lessons to be learnt through MARS

(iii) Keep port records for repeat visits

(iv) Keep navigational publications up to date

(v) Keep navigation files and circulars up to date

(vi) Have review procedure for updating company instructions

(vii) Hold seminars when necessary to obtain fleet advice on navigational policy changes.

Social and technical evaluation

The flag administration is required under Solas to investigate serious accidents. They are the only organisations with the authority to obtain disclosure of information.

The public inquiry is an essential part of navigational safety to:

(a) Discover what happened.

(b) Introduce changes at governmental and international level.

(c) Satisfy the public that their concerns are being safeguarded.

(d) Provide the basis for disciplinary action in the event of negligence or improper conduct.

This system of checks and balances might appear to be over elaborate, but what it does is keep navigational issues to the fore and ensures that standards are maintained and accidents minimised.

Of course, as soon as reliable performance is established the cost of providing a high level of stability is questioned, and if there are no persuasive arguments to keep it, then gradually the system may deteriorate. First it may be sub-contracting, then sub-contracting on cost alone; then, typically, attitudes change and the argument is developed that navigators are paid to navigate and if they cannot do it, new people who can will be found. In going down this path, companies have to rely on the capability of their senior staff more and more. Junior staff coming from a variety of untested backgrounds may be unreliable and certainly there is little appreciation of the hazards should senior officers make a mistake.

Any organisation which aspires to a quality service needs its staff to be able to suggest and implement improvements. Such companies can only do that if they have a good corporate/ship memory. The more distant historical awareness, the more convenient it is not to bother to question incidents major or minor.

Navigators are therefore more likely to reproduce mistakes or inappropriate methods of working; in so doing they inhibit the ability to pass on a corporate culture to the next generation and with it corporate loyalty, professionalism, pride, motivation and a sense of identity. This in turn adversely affects attitudes towards enterprise, work and money. As Arnold Knansdorff observed[19] in a perceptive study in *How to be wise after the event* 'Companies have to re-think their attitudes to nurturing and using their history in all its forms'.

In the quest to make improvements the shipping industry is faced with a dilemma. In many companies they have abandoned their nautical 'memory'. They have employed navigators whom they no longer control through third parties, and there are weaknesses in bridge manning which may not become apparent until there is an accident.

What therefore can be done about this? The Council of The Nautical Institute took the view that nautical people must take responsibility for maintaining and promoting the nautical discipline—nobody else is likely to do so. The Institute initiated the Bridge Operations programme (see Annex II) which was introduced by Mr W. A. O'Neil, Secretary General of the IMO, with these words:

> *Supporting the human element, demands long term commitment which is likely to be most effective, if it provides a common sense of purpose amongst the bridge team.*

The purpose of the programme is to try and re-establish what should be done. To provide a professional, well-documented set of values and practices which can be argued for in the board rooms of companies and across the negotiating table, and with sub-contractors. They are standards which can be applied on board and used for training. In so doing, the Institute is re-asserting professional values which it is hoped will be re-infused into company cultures.

What are acceptable standards?

The IMO has provided the International Regulations for Preventing Collisions at Sea, requirements for those in control of a navigational watch, resolutions concerning safe watchkeeping practices at sea at anchor and in port. It has also developed model courses which specify what should be taught and learnt with respect to navigation, radar use and seamanship. What the IMO does not do and cannot do is put all the elements together, instil judgement and ensure that good intentions are not undermined by bad practices at sea.

In preparing for this paper the author consulted most of the major text books on navigation and, whilst they contain excellent technical advice, none of them dealt with the role of bridge organisation.

This has now been well covered in Captain A. J. Swift's excellent book on *Bridge Team Management* and is a major component of the Institute's Bridge Operations Programme. The book covers such subjects as: error chains; appraisal and passage planning; situational awareness; executing the plan; monitoring progress; team work; navigating with the pilot on board.

Collision avoidance is a peculiarly awkward subject to teach and learn. The ColRegs themselves are reasonable, but their application requires judgement, an appreciation of movement, the ability correctly to assess risk and confident strategies for avoiding close quarters situations. Again, only so much can be learnt in a classroom and advice is needed on how to manage traffic situations on the bridge with the equipment available.

Undoubtedly, radar simulation has been one of the most effective teaching aids, yet this does not provide the appropriate response for vessels in sight of one another. Computer-based training schemes have a real application here and the Seatrade Award to PC Maritime for its bridge watchkeeping package was well deserved. This programme covers:

- The direction of up to nine different target vessels exhibiting all the correct lights, signals and manoeuvring characteristics in accordance with the Regulations.

- The trainee controls own vessel and can be in visual or radar mode. The PC display has a complete set of bridge instruments including relative motion radar with reflective plotter.

- The software consists of two programmes, the OOW course designer, and the OOW simulator.

What this comprehensive simulation provides is not only confirmation of correct identification and heading of vessels for knowledge testing but also an interactive display in which the OOW has to exercise judgement and the ability to apply the rules correctly.

The system is not cheap. Good software has to be paid for, but the package enables companies and training establishments to learn, refresh, test out situations and involve groups in training exercises which can be printed out so also offering the opportunity for analysis and discussion.

Apart from the government surveyor conducting an oral examination (and many adminstrations do not even do this) with models, trainee watchkeepers can go through life not realising that they have a mistaken understanding of the Rules. With good computer-based training, such omissions can be overcome.

Overriding power of industrial employment

It would be wrong to assume that the excellent work carried out by the International Chamber of Shipping through the *Bridge Procedure Guide*, The Nautical Institute Bridge Operations Programme or the resolutions of the IMO and recommendations of government will solve all bridge problems. The fact is that company organisation has a much greater influence on individuals than peripheral outside interests.

The main reason is that behaviour in companies is influenced directly by managers who control employment and pay. Also, people working together exert significantly more peer group pressure on each other than individuals working independently, and this applies particularly to crews. For this reason it is essential that managers understand fully the types of risks they may be taking by failing to have a consistent navigational policy and strategy. It is essential to question and identify areas of doubt.

Is there doubt about what goes on onboard ship? Are the practices safe or have they become degraded? Are there doubts about the ability of individuals and are there doubts about whether the navigators actually are aware of shortcomings in their own systems, procedures, practices and operations?

If there are doubts, there is only one satisfactory way to find out the answers and that is to evaluate *actual performance* either onboard or through simulation. This is the only practical way of creating the situations where bridge team management can be tested.

If bridge team simulation is used it needs to be conducted by fully competent instructors, otherwise bad habits will be re-enforced, but it is probably the most effective measure that can be deployed to create the awareness of potentially dangerous practices, to reaffirm good navigational methods and procedures; to identify weaknesses which might be overcome with further training; to improve communications on the bridge; to use resources more effectively and in so doing, reduce the risk of navigational incidents.

Conclusion

The shipping industry is highly competitive; in most sectors it is overtonnaged and operating margins are slim. Operational costs are all increasing, but revenue remains stubbornly flat. Accidents need to be avoided but resources for accident prevention are under pressure.

Collisions and strandings must not be considered simply as industrial accidents as they have the potential to cause ruin.

A company can build up a safe system of navigational control over time. However, if there is too much change nobody in the organisation may have a true understanding of the risks inherent until there is an accident.

Where there is doubt, the best way of finding out about weakness is through simulated exercises.

Seastaff can then be involved in defining company navigational safety policies and where possible pilots should be encouraged to participate in bridge team training. Investment in this type of training is likely to be cost effective.

However, perhaps the first question which should be asked is: 'Whose actions have the greatest influence on navigational safety?' If the person or persons so indentified are not contributing to the standards necessary, then they need to be told.

Generally, there is need to promote more awareness of effective navigational practices at all levels within the industry so that there is greater mutual under-standing when personnel are assigned to different ships.☐

References

1. *The Institute of London Underwriters Annual Report 1992.*

2. The E C Study COST 301 *Seaways* April 1987.

3. *Ship Costs: Their Structure and Significance,* Drewry 1990.

4. Analysis of Claims, *UK P&I Club Report 1992.*

5. Loss prevention, report to the International Union of Marine Insurance, D. J. Mackenzie, *Seaways,* The Nautical Institute October 1990.

6. Inquiry into the stranding of the LNG Carrier *El Paso Paul Kayser* Liberian Government 1979.

7. Inqury into the stranding of the *Exxon Valdez,* NSTB USA 1989.

8. Inquiry into the stranding of the *Sundancer* Canadian Government 1984.

9. Inquiry into the collision between the *European Gateway* and *Speedlink Vanguard* UK Government 1983.

10. Inquiry into the collision between the *Nordpol* and HMCS *Kootenay,* Canadian Government 1989.

11. Confidential Marine Accident Reporting Scheme. The Nautical Institute, published monthly in *Seaways.*

12. Institute of Shipping Logistics, Analysis of casualties from the German Authorities 1987-1991. *Navigator* May 1993.

13. *The Human Element in Shipping Casualties,* Marine Directorate, UK Department of Transport, HMSO 1991.

14. *Marine Education and Training Examination and Certification of Deck Officers.* M. A. Aziz 1990.

15. *A Survey of Mariners Understanding of Rule 19,* R. Syms, Australian Maritime College 1991.

16. Communication Problems inherent in a Cross Cultural Manning Environment, D. H. Moreby, *Management of Safety in Shipping,* Nautical Institute 1991.

17. *Bridge Watchkeeping a Nautical Briefing* by the Council of The Nautical Institute 1993.

ANNEX 1

Module 1   Model Course for Master and Chief Mate
Navigation—106 hours

Scope

This syllabus covers the requirements of the 1978 STCW Convention, regulation II/2, appendix, paragraphs 2(a) and 2(b)(i) and (ii), and the recommendations in the IMO/ILO Document for Guidance, 1985, sections 3 and 6.

The module covers the theory and practice of navigation necessary for the effective and safe navigation of a ship in coastal waters and in the open sea, including voyage planning and position determination, with emphasis on possible errors and tides. The use of electronic navigational aids and radar is dealt with in module 3, Electronic Navigational Aids, and of compasses in module 4, Magnetic and Gyro-compasses, but references to their use will be made in this course where appropriate.

Sound navigational watchkeeping practices are emphasized by references to regulation II/1 of the 1978 STCW Convention and to resolution 1 of the STW Conference, where applicable.

Objective

On completion of the module, the trainee will possess a thorough understanding and capability in the subject of navigation. His understanding of this subject, together with knowledge gained in other areas, will enable him to carry out passages independently in a proper and safe manner and to be able to solve those problems that may rise during a voyage.

The trainee will be able to fix positions and analyse in a practical way the quality of the fix, do great-circle calculations, read the tide tables and do prediction calculations for a port.

In voyage planning, the trainee will be able to:

- use appropriate means of navigation in coastal waters

- make use of publications and other information sources for safe voyage planning in coastal waters

- use pilot charts, *Ocean Passages for the World* and other publications to choose a safe and economic 'best' route.

Subject outline

- Position determination; terrestrial navigation, great-circle sailing, celestial navigation, tides.

- Voyage planning; coastal navigation, ocean voyage.

Module 2   Watchkeeping—48 hours

Scope

The syllabus covers the requirements of the 1978 STCW Convention, regulation II/2, appendix, paragraph 3, and the recommendations in the IMO/ILO Document for Guidance, 1985, sections 2 and 19.

Objective

On completion of the module, trainees will be thoroughly conversant with the International Regulations for Preventing Collisions at Sea (ColReg 1972) and interpretations of them arising from court decisions. They will be able to apply them correctly and efficiently, in all situations, as master of a ship.

Trainees will be able to arrange and monitor the keeping of a safe navigational watch at sea and an effective deck watch in port, taking full account of the nature of any hazardous cargo or special circumstances on board or ashore. In consultation with the chief engineer officer, they will arrange for the maintenance of appropriate and effective engineering watches for the purposes of safety, at sea and in port.

Trainees will also be conversant with the precautions to be taken by the master to prevent operational and accidental pollution of the environment.

Subject Outline

- Watchkeeping arrangements and procedures; content, application and intent of ColReg 1972, adequacy of navigational watch, exchange of information between master and pilot, adequacy of an engineering watch.

- Keeping a watch in port; deck and engineering watches under normal conditions, deck and engineering watches when carrying hazardous cargo.

- Prevention of pollution; precautions to prevent operational pollution, precautions to prevent accidential pollution, reporting of incidents.

Comment

Note the emphasis on individual capability and the lack of training in pilotage techniques. This makes it difficult to reinforce good team work.

CC

THE NAUTICAL INSTITUTE
ON
BRIDGE OPERATIONS

THE following books, videos and briefings may be purchased separately or together,

BOOK

BRIDGE TEAM MANAGEMENT This practical guide is designed to enhance standards of bridge team management with the purpose of demonstrating effective practices which are necessary to avoid navigational errors. The book covers team management; error chains; casualties and their causes; groundings and their causes; bridge organisation; passage planning; plan execution; monitoring the ship's progress; teamwork; navigation under pilotage; and navigational technology and the human interface.

The book is written by **Captain A.J. Swift**, MNI, a shipmaster who has spent 15 years training bridge teams on the simulator at the Maritime Operations Centre at Warsash. The book was published in July 1993, price £15 (NI Members); £21.43 (non-members).

VIDEOS

The Nautical Institute is supporting the production of three training videos which are being made by Videotel Marine International.

BRIDGE WATCHKEEPING PROCEDURES: This video is designed to reinforce good bridge watchkeeping practices.

PASSAGE PLANNING: This video is designed to demonstrate the need to prepare passages in advance, berth to berth, with the overall objective of giving the watchkeeping officer a plan to follow and sufficient information to enable him to do that easily.

THE MASTER/PILOT RELATIONSHIP: This video recognises that the master and pilot are two professionals with a common purpose. It discusses responsibilities, the exchange of information and ways of ensuring the best basis for a safe passage through busy confined and sometimes hazardous waters.

Information concerning these three videos, which are due to be produced during 1993, can be obtained directly from Videotel Productions, Ramilles House, 1-2 Ramilles Street, London W1V 1DF, UK: Tel: 071-439 6301.

ON-BOARD TRAINING MANUAL

BRIDGE WATCHKEEPING: This is a training manual with a difference. It is written in open learning format with principles and practices well illustrated with diagrams. It is produced for the guidance of junior watchkeeping officers and trainees.

OBJECTIVES

On completion of the study programme contained in the book the junior officer should have a better understanding of:
A The stages of the passage and the structure of the bridge watchkeeping organisation.
B The watchkeeping tasks of the bridge officer.
C The role of the bridge equipment.
D The professional relationship between the master and the bridge watchkeeping officers.

CONTENTS

1. Introduction to bridge watchkeeping procedures.
2. The stages of the passage.
3. Preparing for sea.
4. Alongside the berth/at anchor.
5. Embarking the pilot/updating the plan.
6. Undocking/weighing anchor.
7. Narrow Waters.
8. Disembarking the pilot.
9. Coastal waters.
10. Ocean areas.
11. Making a landfall/preparing for arrival/docking.
12. Professional relationship between master and bridge watchkeeping officer.

This book draws upon existing regulations and codes as the basis of the text. It is being written by **Captain H.H. Francis**, MNI, and **Captain T.C. Rooney**, BSc, FNI, and verified by the Isle of Man Branch. The manual is due to be published in December 1993 price approx £15.

– –

If you would like more information when these publications become available please write or fax to **Mrs. J.E. Miller, Publications Officer (Fax 071 401 2537), The Nautical Institute, 202 Lambeth Road, London SE1 7LQ, UK.**

Name: ....

Address: ....

....

....

Your Fax No: ....

I would be interested in bulk order rates.

Please send me information
when available of

☐ **BRIDGE TEAM MANAGEMENT**

☐ **BRIDGE VIDEOS**

☐ **BRIDGE WATCHKEEPING MANUAL**

☐

FACING RISING CARGO CLAIMS WITH A NEW APPROACH TO LOSS PREVENTION

Philip Anderson, Master Mariner, BA (Hons), FNI

Liaison and Training Executive, North of England P&I Association

Philip Anderson

PHILIP ANDERSON commenced his seagoing career in 1969 as a cadet with the Bibby Line of Liverpool. He remained with the Bibby Line throughout his seagoing career, serving on board general-cargo vessels, bulk carriers, OBOs, liquid gas carriers and container vessels. He came ashore in 1980, after obtaining his Class 1 Master Mariners Certificate, and took up a career as a P&I claims executive with the Sunderland P&I Association.

In 1987, he transferred to the North of England P&I Association in a similar capacity. In 1991, Mr Anderson was appointed to a unique new position in the P&I industry as liaison and training executive of the North of England P&I Association, responsible for all education and training and loss prevention initiatives and monitoring services provided by lawyers, surveyors and correspondents.

He is currently Vice-Chairman of the North East Branch of The Nautical Institute and chaired the North East Branch Committee producing the book *The Masters Role in Collecting Evidence*. Chairman of The Nautical Institute sub-committee organising annual seminars specifically geared towards the serving seafarer on the general theme 'The Mariner and the Maritime Law'.

Mr Anderson was elected a fellow of The Nautical Institute. He acted as technical editor and chairman of joint venture between the North of England P&I Association and the South Tyneside College, producing a distance learning course in P&I insurance. He is the author of the North of England P&I Association Report *The Human Element in Claims—What Role for the P&I Clubs?*

Facing Rising Cargo Claims with a New Approach to Loss Prevention

APPENDICES

Acknowledgements

The United Kingdom Mutual Steamship Assurance Association (Bermuda) Ltd.

- *Analysis of Major Claims 1992.*

The North of England Protecting and Indemnity Association Ltd.

- The Human Element in Claims—What Role for the P&I Clubs?
- Loss Prevention Newsletter *Signals* Vol 3 No. 1 January, 1993.
- Tally Schedule—Bagged Cargoes.
- *The North of England P&I Association Rule Book 1993.*
- A Distance Learning Course in P&I Insurance—2nd Edition—1992.

Nautical Institute

- *The Masters Role in Collecting Evidence—1989.*

United Nations

- The Hamburg Rules.

Captain John Knott

- Weather-Deck Steel Hatch Covers plus some photographs and diagrams.

Columbia Shipmanagement Ltd. and Seatrade Review 1993

- Daily Budget Graphs.

West of England P&I Association

- *West of England Annual Review 1992.*

The Britannia Steamship Insurance Association Ltd.

- *Britannia News* Number 17, July 1992.

HMSO

- Carriage of Goods by Sea Act 1971.
- *Safety Aspects of Ship Design and Technology*—House of Lords—Select Committee on Science and Technology—1992.
- *The Human Element in Shipping Casualties*—Marine Directorate Department of Transport—1991.

1.0.0. Introduction

In order to understand the significance of rising cargo claims and why it is felt necessary to put forward a 'new' approach to loss prevention it is important to appreciate a number of related issues.

First of all it is important to understand the relevance of cargo claims to a shipowner's operation. Clearly a prudent cargo owner insures his cargo but shipowners are not cargo underwriters. Why should a shipowner be concerned?

Secondly the phenomenal rise in claims of all types, and cargo claims specifically, which have occurred in the last seven years or so needs to be examined. During this period claims have risen by approximately 300%. Why has this occurred? What are the underlying causes? What sort of claims have arisen?

Finally the question needs to be asked: Why have these claims arisen? and what, if anything, can be done to prevent these claims arising?

This paper will attempt to explore these issues. This will not be easy for there are many different factors affecting the rise in the number, size and complexity of claims, on the one hand and, on the other hand a fairly radical change in the way in which ships are operated may be needed if the problem of rising claims is to be dealt with effectively.

Having said that, though, there is, in reality, little which will be 'new' at all. Indeed quite the contrary, much of what will be said is nothing more than common sense and, if the cliche will be excused, and without wishing to over simplify the problem, it will be a matter of doing things as they were done in the 'good-old-days!' This may, at first glance, appear to be a vague sentimentality or maybe a utopian pipe dream; and the critic would no doubt say that we cannot turn the clock back—that the difficult market conditions which exist in shipping today are not conducive to some high ideals which may (or may not) have existed in the past. The reality is that the difficult market conditions are being made much more difficult for shipowners and operators because the amount of money they are having to spend on insurance costs— which are a direct result of rising claims— have risen by 300 to 400% in many cases during the last few years. In some cases nearly half of the ship's operating costs are used to buy insurance! How much longer can shipowners continue to fund these rising insurance costs?

Most people will be aware that the commercial insurance companies and individual underwriters at Lloyd's for example have faced enormous losses in recent years. They are in business to make a profit and hence, if they continue to underwrite marine business, their insurance premiums will continue to rise. The P&I Clubs operate on a non-profit making basis but clearly they cannot make a loss either and so their 'calls' and supplementary calls will continue to rise.

There is a 'law' in philosophy, which goes back many hundreds of years, and often referred to as 'Ockham's Razor' (after William of Ockham who was a monk living around 1300), which basically says that if you have tried and tested system which works well then there is little point searching for an alternative.

Clearly a more open minded approach to today's problem is needed, but if, at the end of the day no realistic or viable alternative to solve the problem is found then, it is suggested, it would not be illogical to re-examine objectively the original method of dealing with the problem and ask why such a system cannot be reintroduced and what the alternatives will be if the opportunity is lost.

During the course of this paper many recent publications, reports, statistics, etc. will be referred to. One report in particular will be referred to extensively— *The United Kingdom P&I Club's Analysis of Major Claims 1992* from which numerous statistics will be quoted. This is not only a very well researched, presented and comprehensive report but is also, probably, a very good indicator as to what is happening throughout the industry. The UK Club is the largest P&I Club and provides P&I cover for approximately 25% of all the deep sea shipping of the world fleet. Other large P&I Clubs who have subsequently carried out their own research seem to confirm, and in some cases almost mirror, the results and conclusions arrived at by the UK Club. It is, therefore, a very good and authoritative reference source.

1.1.0. Basically English Law position adopted

It should be stated, at this early stage, that, because of the background of the writer, the interpretation and views expressed in this paper are very much based upon the English Law position. However, because of the generality of many of the issues discussed it would be fair to say that the views expressed could apply to many non-English regimes. This will not always be the case. For example in some Islamic countries the Sharia Law and the Holy Koran may take precedence over any commercial law. Some caution therefore may need to be exercised.

1.2.0. Cargo insurance—P&I insurance (Why a shipowner is concerned)

It may not be obvious to some people why a shipowner should be involved with cargo claims. If there is damage to the cargo, or if there is a shortage in outturn, then the cargo owner would, in the normal course of events, look to his cargo underwriter for compensation. After all, he will have paid his insurance premium to cover these very risks.

However, the shipowner is very much involved. As a carrier the shipowner becomes, in legal terms, a bailee of the cargo. The cargo owners have entrusted their cargo into the safe keeping of the shipowner to transport it from load port to destination. There is a legal obligation upon the carrier to deliver the cargo at destination in the same good order and condition, and quantity, as it was in when loaded.

The shipowner therefore is not acting as an insurer of the cargo, but rather he owes a duty of care to the cargo owner and if the cargo is lost or damaged whilst in his custody, then he will be obliged to compensate the cargo owner, unless he can invoke one of the exceptions as contained in the Hague Rules for example, or otherwise prove that the loss or damage did not occur as a result of any fault on the part of the shipowner.

What usually happens in practice is that the cargo owner is insured. He claims from his insurance company for any loss or damage to his cargo and the insurance company is then subrogated to the rights of the insured and pursues a recovery against the carrier— usually the shipowner.

The shipowner is insured for these and other third party liability risks with a Protecting and Indemnity Association (or P&I Club as it is more usually called).

1.3.0.Function of a merchant vessel

What must never be lost sight of is the fact that the main function of most merchant vessels is to carry cargo from the port of loading to destination—it is part of a commercial venture. The aim of that commercial venture, as far as the shipowner is concerned is to make, or try to make, a profit.

The employment of people, both ashore and on board, the compliance with all the various rules and regulations, the necessity to maintain the ship in class and pay insurance premiums and everything else which a shipowner does, all flow from this basic function. The wages bill, the insurance premium, the cost of maintenance etc., etc., all have to be found by the shipowner from the remuneration he might receive from carrying out this basic function of transporting cargoes. This may appear to be stating the obvious, but it sometimes seems that that simple reality is lost sight of.

Shipowners do not have bottomless pockets—they are business people and most of them are responsible, but trying to operate their ships in a very depressed market with very little return.

The temptation is always there though to cut costs wherever possible—this is often at the expense of quality crews and/or maintenance. It is suggested that this is a short-term and short-sighted policy, for it will inevitably lead to increased claims which, in turn, will lead to increased insurance costs.

This paper will attempt to put forward an alternative solution to avoid this downward spiral. By investing in people, claims and the resulting insurance costs will be reduced, which will increase the possibility of a profitable, commercial venture.

The most common type of third party liability claim which a shipowner has to face is cargo claims. This category of claim will therefore be used as the basis for discussion in this paper, but it must be recognised that the solving of one category of claim in isolation will not solve the whole problem of rising claims. It is suggested, however, that many of the solutions put forward in the paper will have relevance to other categories of claim.

1.4.0 Responsibility of the carrier

Throughout the latter half of the 19th century there was increasing dissatisfaction amongst cargo owners and their insurers with the law governing a carrier's liabilities for damage to goods in their custody. This was due to an increasing number of protection and other limitation clauses in the contract which substantially reduced the cargo liabilities of carriers.

There was a growing demand to establish a uniform code of rules for the carriage of goods by sea. After many years of talking between the shipowners and

underwriters, a conference on maritime law was eventually held at Brussels in 1922 which resulted in a set of rules known as the Hague Rules being adopted as the basis of a draft convention. The international convention was signed by many participating countries at Brussels in 1924. In the United Kingdom the rules were incorporated in the Carriage of Goods by Sea Act 1924.

The aim of the Hague Rules was to establish a uniform code for the carriage of cargo shipped under bills of lading. States adopting the rules usually apply them as a matter of law for cargoes exported from that State.

In 1968, the Hague Rules were revised and amended in order to bring them into line with the needs of the modern shipping industry.

The amended rules are known as the Hague Visby Rules and are, broadly speaking, similar to the Hague Rules. In the United Kingdom the Hague Visby Rules were incorporated in the Carriage of Goods by Sea Act 1971.

1.4.1 Under the Hague/Hague Visby regime

The Hague/Hague Visby Rules impose certain responsibilities and duties on the carrier. The main provisions are set out in Article III Rules 1 and 2 which read as follows:

ARTICLE III

1. The carrier shall be bound before and at the beginning of the voyage to exercise due diligence to:

(a) Make the ship seaworthy.
(b) Properly man, equip and supply the ship.
(c) Make the holds, refrigerating and cool chambers, and all other parts of the ship in which goods are carried, fit and safe for their reception, carriage and preservation.

2. Subject to the provisions of Article IV, the carrier shall properly and carefully load, handle, stow, carry, keep, care for, and discharge the goods carried.

1.4.2.Under the Hamburg Rules

A further convention on the Carriage of Goods by Sea was held in Hamburg in 1978. The provisions agreed at this convention are known as the Hamburg Rules.

Whereas the Hague and Hague Visby Rules represent a balance between the carrier's responsibilities and his rights and immunities, the Hamburg Rules do not follow this philosophy. Instead, the Hamburg Rules makes the presumption that the carrier is responsible for any loss or damage unless it is proved that the carrier took all measures that could reasonably be required, to avoid the occurrence and its consequences.

At least 20 countries were needed to ratify the 1978 convention; on 7 October 1991 the twentieth ratification was received and, as a consequence, the Hamburg Rules entered into force on 1 November 1992.

Scope of application—Article 2

The rules apply to the carriage of goods by sea governed by a contract of carriage, other than charter-parties. Not only do the rules apply if the contractual port of loading or discharging is in a Hamburg Rules State but also if the bill of lading, or other contractual document, is issued in a Hamburg Rules State.

Article 1 and 4—The Carrier and Period of Responsibility.

The definition of carrier in the rules is very general, including 'any person by whom or in whose name a contract of carriage of goods by sea has been concluded with a shipper' and no distinction is made between shipowners and charterers. A further distinction is made between carrier and actual carrier, who is the party to whom the performance of the contract has been entrusted.

A carrier is responsible for the goods throughout the entire period as opposed to the Hague—Hague Visby system where the carrier is responsible from the point of loading to the point of discharge. This means that the carrier, will be generally responsible once he takes over the goods at the port of loading until handing them over at the port of discharge. This could vary, however, depending on the laws, regulations and usages of the ports in question.

It will be recalled that the Hague and Hague-Visby Rules require the carrier to exercise due diligence to make the vessel seaworthy and cargo worthy before and at the beginning of each voyage. Under the Hamburg Rules the carrier has a duty to make the vessel seaworthy but the concept of exercising due diligence is dropped in favour of one which requires reasonable care to be taken during the entire period when the goods are in the charge of the carrier.

1.4.3. Under a charter party

There are literally hundreds of different charter party forms and it would not be realistically practical to discuss in any sort of detail even a handful of them in a paper such as this.

However, some general comments can be made: There are legally two types of charter party:(1) demise (2) non-demise.

1. Demise charter

A charter by demise is not very common, although one particular species, a 'bare boat' charter is encountered, particularly in the oil trade, or for quasi military purposes.

Under a charter by demise the whole use of the ship passes to the charterer, by reason of the charterer paying all expenses incurred. It is really a complete lease of the ship, with the charterer appointing his own master and crew.

2. Non-demise charter

There are two types of non-demise charters:

(a) Voyage charter

In which the shipowner carries an agreed cargo from a specified port to another specified port for a pre-arranged freight. The majority of tramp cargo shipments are made on a voyage charter basis.

(b) Time charter.

In which the shipowner lets his ship to a charterer for a stated period or voyage for a remuneration known as hire money. The shipowner continues to manage his own vessel under the time charterer's instructions. It is quite common for liner companies to supplement their services by taking tramp ships on time charter.

Hague Rules are not compulsorily applicable to charter parties, but it is not unusual to see them specifically incorporated— usually by way of a clause paramount.

There may be specific clauses which make it quite clear who, as between the shipowner and charterer, is responsible for the loading, stowing and discharging etc., of the cargo and that party would usually be the one ultimately responsible for any loss or damage to the cargo which resulted from those operations. However, the shipowner will usually remain responsible for damage to the cargo which has resulted from some unseaworthiness of the vessel.

1.5.0. Exceptions available to the carrier

The Hague and Hague Visby Rules also set out the carrier's rights and immunities.

The carrier's rights and immunities are set out in Article IV Rule 2 of the Hague/Hague Visby Rules, which will be found set out in 1.5.1. below, but it is important to appreciate the following points:

The carrier must comply with the obligations as to seaworthiness and cargo worthiness imposed by Article III Rules 1 and 2 before being allowed to try to establish that one or other of the exceptions exonerate the carrier from liability, for the loss or damage suffered as set out in Article IV Rule 2.

1.5.1. Under the Hague/Hague Visby regime

The carrier's rights and immunities are set out in Article IV Rule 2; which reads as follows:

ARTICLE IV

2. Neither the carrier nor the ship shall be responsible for loss or damage arising or resulting from—

(a) Act, neglect or default of the Master, mariner, pilot, or the servants of the carrier in the navigation or in the management of the ship.
(b) Fire, unless caused by the actual fault or privity of the carrier.
(c) Perils, dangers and accidents of the sea or other navigable water.
(d) Act of God.
(e) Act of war.
(f) Act of public enemies.
(g) Arrest or restraint of princes, rulers or people, or seizure under legal process.
(h) Quarantine restrictions.
(i) Act or omission of the shipper or owner of the goods, his agent or representative.
(j) Strikes or lockouts or stoppage or restraint of labour from whatever cause, whether partial or general.

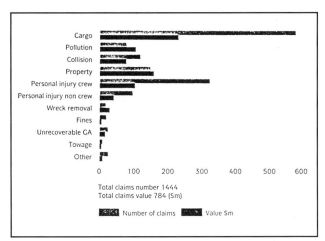

Fig 1: Source—The UK Club analysis of major claims 1992.

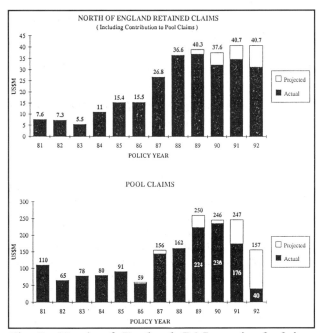

Fig 2: North of England P&I retained claims (including contribution to Pool claims).

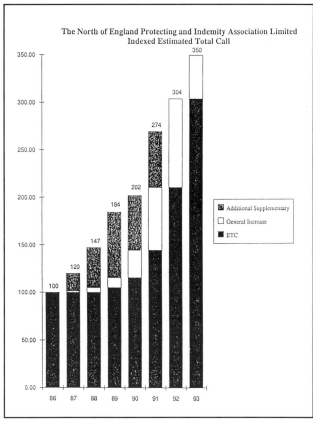

Fig 3: North of England P&I Association Ltd. indexed estimated total call.

Fig 4: Source—Columbia Shipmanagement Ltd, reproduced in Seatrade Review 1993.

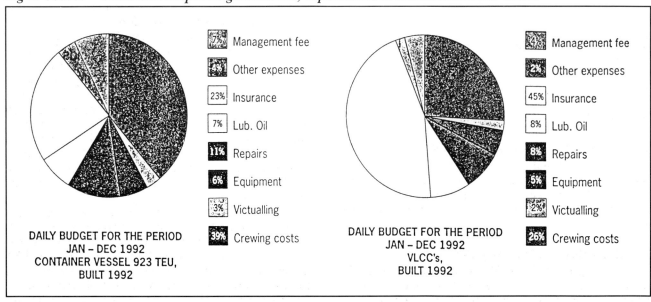

(k) Riots and civil commotions.

(l) Saving or attempting to save life or property at sea.

(m) Wastage in bulk or weight or any other loss or damage arising from inherent defect, quality or vice of the goods.

(n) Insufficiency of packing.

(o) Insufficiency or inadequacy of marks.

(p) Latent defects not discoverable by due diligence.

(q) Any other cause arising without the actual fault or privity of the carrier, or without the fault or neglect of the agents or servants of the carrier, but the burden of proof shall be on the person claiming the benefit of this exception to show that neither the actual fault or privity of the carrier nor the fault or neglect of the agents or servants of the carrier contributed to the loss or damage.

Time limit to bring suit—Article III Rule 6

Under the Hague—Hague Visby Rules owners of the cargo must bring a suit for loss or damage within one year from the time the goods are delivered or should have been delivered, otherwise the carrier is discharged from all liability.

Limitation of liability—Article IV Rule 5

If the carrier is liable for loss or damage to goods the rules allow the carrier to limit this liability on a basis determined solely by the number of packages or units.

1.5.2.Under the Hamburg Rules— Article 5

If goods are lost, damaged or delayed in their delivery the carrier will be liable if the occurrence causing the loss, damages or delay took place whilst the goods were under his charge; there is a presumed fault of the carrier who has no rights and immunities which were afforded by the Hague and Hague Visby Rules (Article IV Rule 2). Under the Hamburg Rules the burden of proof is on the carrier to show that he, his servants or agents took all measures that could reasonably be required to avoid the occurrence and its consequences.

Limitation of action—Article 20

Time limits for actions related to the carriage of goods are extended to two years from the time the goods have been delivered or should have been delivered as against one year in the case of the Hague—Hague Visby Rules.

Limitation of liability—Article 6

If the carrier is liable for the loss or damage to goods the carrier can in a similar way to that afforded by the Hague—Hague Visby Rules, limit this liability to a sum determined by the number of packages or gross weight.

1.5.3.Under a charter party

If the Hague or Hague Visby Rules are specifically incorporated by way of a Clause Paramount, then the usual exceptions will be available to the carrier.

If they are not, then the parties are free to contract as they will. Alternatively, in England for example, the Common Law might apply which provides very few exceptions for the carrier.

The most usual situation though, even where a charter party is in existence, is that the contract of carriage under which cargo claims arise is that evidenced by the bills of lading. Once the claim has been settled under the bill of lading, then the party who has settled will need to look to the terms of the charter party to determine whether he will have a valid indemnity claim against the other party.

2.0.0.Nature of the problem

Within the last decade, there has been an explosion in the area of third party liability claims against shipowners. The largest proportion of these claims, both in number and in quantum, were cargo related claims.

Figure 1 (page 46) provides an indication of the distribution of major claims by risk type. A similar graph of smaller claims would suggest an even more significant differential of cargo claims as against other types of claims.

2.1.0.Significant rise in the number, size and complexity of claims in recent years

The year 1987 is often seen as the time when the 'claims explosion' occurred. Certainly that was the year when the insurance world first seemed to 'get their sums wrong', with some clubs starting to call very large 'supplementaries'.

On the face of it, there certainly seems to have been a very significant rise in the number, size and complexity of claims in that year and this trend has continued upwards on an almost exponential curve.

There has been much written about the possible causes of this phenomena; much debate and little agreement. One thing that most would agree on though is that there was no single cause. Certainly it coincided, with a time-lag element, to the change in management practices and the shift from employing the more traditional (and usually more expensive) nationalities of seafarer, to the less traditional (and usually less expensive) labour force.

Without doubt, during this period, the average age of the world fleet was increasing and there was little new building taking place. Freight rates and charter hire rates were depressed and, as a consequence, some shipowners were cutting back on their maintenance budgets. For similar reasons, the training budgets in some fleets were cut back or disappeared altogether. No doubt there were many other contributing factors.

One aspect which may not be generally appreciated is that the apparent escalation in claims is actually a result of the way in which a P&I Club carries out its underwriting.

It will not be realistic to discuss in any detail the intricacies of P&I underwriting principles. However, it may be sufficient to say that P&I underwriting is 'reactive' in nature, rather than 'proactive'. The P&I underwriter would look at past claims experience and trends in order to predict what sort of premium, or more correctly 'call' should be made in the future.

What, perhaps, had not been taken fully into account, was the fact that in the early part of the 1980s and indeed the late 1970s, there was a significant amount of tonnage in lay-up. Clearly, in this quiescent state, claims were not being generated—cargoes were not being carried. However, by the mid-1980s a fairly extensive reactivation programme was underway— the ships were trading again—they were carrying cargo again, and having cargo claims again!

It is suggested that if P&I underwriting had been proactive, rather than reactive, then it would have recognised the propensity for these ships coming out of lay-up to experience claims and would have made an appropriate allowance in the calculation of the 'call' income required, rather than surprise the shipowners with very large and unexpected supplementary calls.

2.2.0.Rising costs of P&I insurance

From their earliest days, P&I Clubs have been mutual, non-profit making organisations. Whilst they cannot make a profit, clearly they cannot be allowed to make a loss. Each year, the P&I Club will need to 'call' in from its shipowner members sufficient money to pay all the justified liability claims brought against its membership, plus an amount to cover managerial and administration expenses and to reinsure the larger claims.

This is very different from the commercial insurance market where the insurance company calculates the risk, charges what it sees as an appropriate fixed premium and, if it finds that there are less claims than the premium figure, then it has made a profit; if the claims exceed the premium, then the insurance company will have to try and recover its losses in subsequent years.

The P&I Club's books need to balance each and every year. In order to achieve this, the shipowner is told at the beginning of the policy year what the club believes the 'call' will be, the estimated total call (ETC). The shipowner then pays a percentage of that figure at the beginning of the policy year, or by instalments throughout the year. At the end of the first year, and at regular intervals after that for maybe three years or more, the policy year and 'actual' claims experience is reviewed and, if it is worse than expected, then additional supplementary calls are made upon the shipowner membership to produce sufficient money to balance the books. (As a corollary if the initial calculation or ETC had been too high, then any surplus funds would be paid back to the shipowner members, or go to build up a reserve fund to ease the burden on poorer years).

It can perhaps be seen from figures 2 and 3 (page 46) which show the increases experienced by the North of England P&I Association (which performed better than most) and the increase in International Group Pool Claims, how these rising costs which are a direct result of rising claims, have escalated upwards since the mid-1980s.

There is a misconception which seems to exist in the mind of some people that a shipowner is insured for these sorts of third party liability risks and therefore it doesn't matter too much if he suffers a claim or two. From the above it should be very clear that it matters a great deal, for any increase in claims means that the shipowner has to pay more to the general fund in the short term and will have his claims record affected, which means he will pay even more in the long term.

2.3.0.Significance to a shipowner

We must never lose sight of the fact that operating ships is a commercial venture. Like any business enterprise, the shipowner expects to make a profit from the trading of his ships, whether he be chartering his ships out or operating in the liner trade. Increasing claims mean ever increasing insurance costs.

A decade ago, a shipowner could expect his total insurance expense, P&I and Hull & Machinery, to account for something like 10% or less of his total operating budget. Recent figures suggest that the total insurance costs of some shipowners has risen to about 45% of the total operating costs—see figure 4 (page 46). To say that this is significant and alarming would be an understatement!

During this period, charter-hire and freight rates— i.e. the return which a shipowner should expect—have remained severely depressed throughout the range of the shipping markets.

One does not need to be an economics genius to work out that the financial significance to a shipowner is horrendous.

There are many factors affecting the actual contribution each individual shipowner pays to his P&I Club by way of 'call'. There are such things as age, size and type of vessel which are taken into account when calculating the appropriate contribution. There is the trading pattern and nationality of the crew to consider and, indeed, a number of other factors.

However, the most significant factor is the past claims record. A shipowner with an excellent claims record would contribute substantially less than a shipowner operating an identical ship in all respects, but with a bad claims record.

What must be appreciated is that the very livelihood of those employed by the shipowner depends upon the success and viability of the commercial venture. It is therefore of immediate concern to all those involved to reduce claims as much as is humanly possible!

Some examples will perhaps help to illustrate the point. Whilst these examples are hypothetical, they are not unrealistic.

Estimated total call comparison

		1986/1987	1993/1994
1.	General Cargo Vessel Built 1976—GRT 9,500 with poor claims record	US$ 12,000	US$110,000
2.	Bulk Carrier Built 1970— GRT 30,000 with very bad claims record	US$ 35,000 (this also includes an increase in deductible to US$500,000)	US$190,000
3.	General Cargo Vessel Built 1976— GRT 5,500 with an improving claims record	US$ 20,000	US$ 65,000
4.	Bulk Carrier Built 1982— GRT 36,000 with a good claims record	US$ 31,000	US$ 66,000

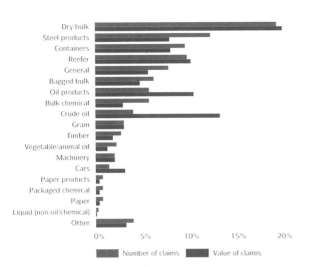

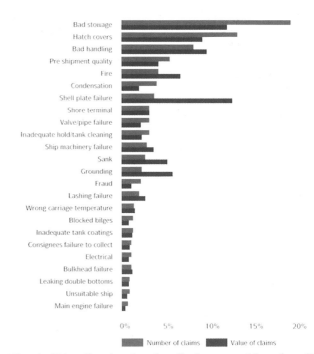

Fig. 5: Distribution of claims by cargo type—source, the UK Club analysis of major claims 1992

Fig 6: Distribution by type of loss for nine selected cargoes (UK Club 1992).

Fig. 7: Distribution by detailed cause of loss for all cargoes (UK Club 1992).

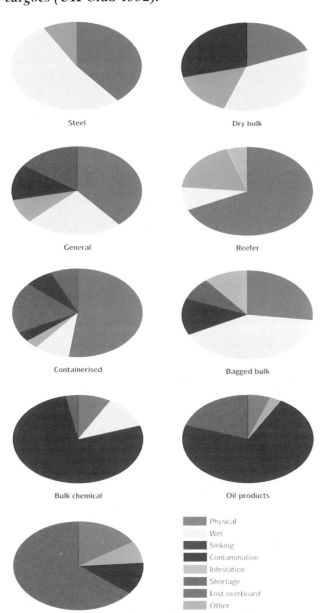

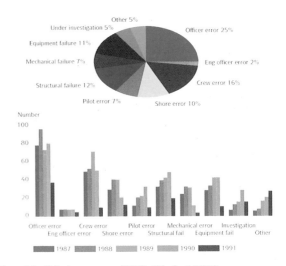

Fig. 14: Main cause (UK Club 1992).

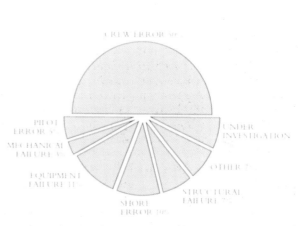

Fig 15: Primary causes—source, West of England annual review 1992.

Fig 8: Wetting of cargo due to leaking hatch covers.

Fig 9: One container crashes on another.

Fig 10: Consequences of inadequate stowage.

2.4.0. Problem not restricted to less traditional maritime nations

It is not uncommon to hear accusations made against certain flag States, or nationalities or flag of convenience ships as being the ones with the major problems, or experiencing the highest incidence of claims. The writer is unaware of any statistical or documented evidence which would support such an accusation as far as liability claims are concerned. Indeed, from his own experience of handling P&I claims for many years, and from the result of recent research he undertook—*The Human Element in Claims—What Role for the P&I Clubs?*—it would appear that the problem of claims affects ships of the so-called traditional maritime nations in a similar way to the ships of the not-so traditional maritime nations. There are perhaps a number of reasons for this which will be explored further in section 3 below.

2.5.0. The future

It may appear a little premature at this stage in this paper to speculate about the future. However, it must be recognised that if the problem of rising claims is not dealt with, and dealt with very quickly, then the costs of insurance will continue to rise and there will come a time, probably in the not too distant future, when the operating costs for the shipowner are so disproportionate to the returns that the venture becomes unviable.

2.6.0. Types of claims arising

Figure 1 provides an indication of the different types of claims which arise. These statistics have been taken from the *UK P&I Club Analysis of Major Claims 1992*. The UK P&I Club is the single biggest P&I Club in which there are entered approximately 25% of the world blue water shipping—the splendid work they have done therefore, with their analysis, probably provides an accurate reflection of the industry generally.

This paper though is primarily concerned with cargo claims. Therefore within the context of this section, the types of cargo claims arising will be analysed and UK P&I Club analysis figures will be relied upon to illustrate the relevant points.

The UK Club analysed 602 major cargo claims (each individual claim had a value in excess of US$100,000) with a total value of US$235 million.

Figure 5 (page 49) shows, for each type of cargo, the number and value of claims as a percentage of all major cargo claims. It will be seen that dry bulk cargoes are the most significant and the UK Club explains that sugar is most often the cargo involved (in about 10% of bulk claims) followed by rice, fishmeal, cement, fertilizer, coffee, grain, and groundnuts (each about 5% of bulk claims).

Another interesting set of diagrams produced by the UK Club is reproduced at figure 6 (page 49) which shows the distribution by type of loss for nine selected cargoes that are most frequently damaged and which, between them, account for more than 80% of the major cargo claims. Further reference to this diagram will be made in the sections 2.6.1.-2.6.8. below, as appropriate.

A more detailed look at causation was made—see figure 7 (page 49)—which shows a percentage distribution, by number and value, of the cause of damage, taking all cargoes into account. With reference to this diagram, the UK Club Report points out that ' . . . bad stowage, preshipment quality disputes, condensation, carriage at the wrong temperature and the use of an unsuitable ship for the cargo in question, together make up about one third of the claims'. They go on to suggest that ' . . . these are all factors to which knowledge of cargoes and stowage is relevant, both on the part of those with immediate responsibility for safe carriage—the ship's master, officers and crew—and on the part of those who fix the ships'.

What should also be mentioned here is that for every 'major' claim there are many more 'minor' claims, but the writer would suggest, from his own claims handling experience, that the overall picture of the 'minor' claims would probably mirror that presented for the 'major' claims.

2.6.1. Shortage claims

If the cargo is accurately measured going into the ship—e.g. by tallying a bagged cargo or conducting an ullage survey on a liquid cargo— a bill of lading is issued stating the quantity thus ascertained and the cargo is accurately measured on outturn, then, in theory, shortages should not occur.

From figure 6 it can be quickly ascertained that shortages seem to be most prolific in liquid oil cargoes—it would seem that about two thirds of all the cargo claims on crude oil are shortages.

Considerable caution should be exercised when drawing conclusions from this particular set of diagrams. It is suggested that if a lower value limit had been imposed on the analysed sample then cargo types such as bagged bulk and dry bulk would show a very much larger percentage of type of loss against the category shortage.

Many of the oil cargo shortage claims have arisen because of inconsistent sets of measurement calculations. The bill of lading may be based on a set of figures supplied by shippers based on measurement of the shore tanks, using one set of tables at one standard temperature and density. The ship's figure based on the ullage survey may differ considerably from the shore figure, and the quantity is then again determined in shore tanks at the receiver's premises—using a different set of tables working at a different standard temperature and density. This is after the oil has been pumped through possibly miles of pipeline ashore. Indeed, ship's personnel are frequently denied access to shore tanks and pipelines to check the measurement and whether the pipes are full or empty of cargo or whether cargo has been 'accidentally' diverted into another tank ashore. It is not at all surprising that apparent shortages arise with such totally unacceptable and inconsistent methods of measuring.

It is suggested that the only consistent method of measuring a bulk liquid cargo is by a detailed on-board ullage survey at loadport and discharge port. With hydrocarbon cargoes it is not unusual to find small apparent losses as a consequence of evaporation, or clingage or inaccurately quantified sediments and

Fig 11: Consequences of inadequate stowage.

Fig 12: More inadequate stowage.

Fig 13: Inadequate stowage yet again.

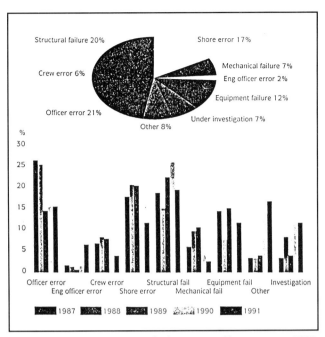

Fig 16: Main cause of damage all cargoes (UK Club 1992).

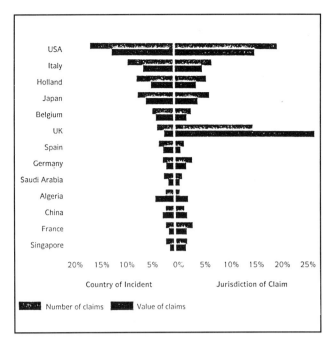

Fig 19: Comparative distribution by country of incident and by jurisdiction of claim (UK Club 1992).

Fig. 18

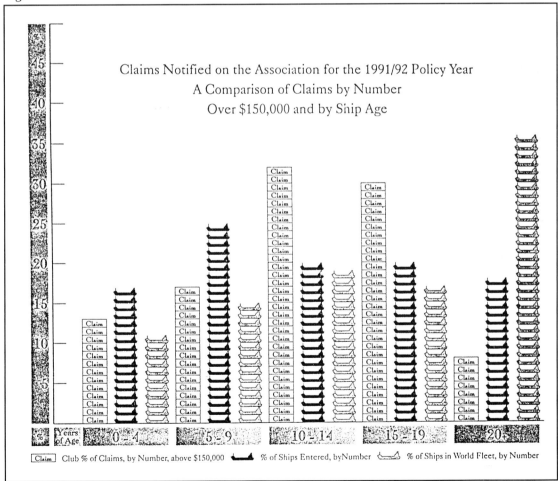

Claims Notified on the Association for the 1991/92 Policy Year
A Comparison of Claims by Number
Over $150,000 and by Ship Age

water contained in the cargo during loading, or indeed, human measuring error. However, such losses should not be held against the carrier and, with the appropriate evidence, the carrier should be in a positon to repudiate such claims. Without the evidence it would be very difficult to successfully defeat a prima facie shortage claim.

Shortages in bagged cargoes, which cannot be satisfactorily defended, have probably come about because the charterers or shippers (who are often the same people) carried out the tally of the bags onto the ship and the cargo receiver tallied the bags out of the ship. There was no contradictory tally at either end by the shipowner. Consequently, without such contemporaneous evidence to challenge the cargo interests' tally figures, which will be reflected in the bill of lading, the shipowners are unlikely to be in a position to successfully defeat such claims. It is very important that the shipowner carries out his own tally of the cargo and ensures that the Master and officers are keeping a very close eye on the tally clerks and cross checking with any other tally that may be taking place.

A useful piece of evidence, which will also help develop good practices, would be a completed Tally Schedule as appears at Appendix 1.

2.6.2. Salt water wetting claims

From diagram 6 it will be seen that the single most significant cause of cargo damage claims on steel, dry bulk, bagged bulk and, to a lesser extent, on general cargo, is wet damage.

It is not clear from the diagram what is actually included as wet damage but, presumably, it includes such things as condensation, shell plate failure, blocked bilges, leaking double bottom as well as hatch cover leakages.

However, figure 7 provides a more detailed breakdown and it can be seen that leaking hatch covers are second only to what is categorised as bad stowage.

Salt water wetting claims no doubt include hatch cover leakages but can include other structural failures which have allowed sea water to enter the cargo compartments. A more detailed discussion of patent steel hatch covers will take place in section 4.3.2., but for the time being suffice to say that cargo damage by seawater ingress through patent steel hatch covers is such a frequently recurring head of claim that there is little excuse when such a claim is presented. Invariably, but not always, an inspection of the leaking hatch covers will reveal poor or inadequate maintenance and/or missing components—and in the worst cases excessive corrosion to the extent of actual holes in the hatch covers.

The vast majority of these salt water wetting claims should never have been carried out on the hatch covers. What may have been saved by cutting back on the hatch cover maintenance probably represents a small percentage of the value of the resulting cargo damage claim.

Wetting of cargo due to leaking hatch covers is well illustrated in figure 8 (page 50). The vertical columns of wet grain are directly below the transverse hatch cover seals.

2.6.3. Contamination claims

Quite understandably, this category of claim is most significant in bulk cargoes whether they be dry or liquid. When a bulk cargo is contaminated it is usually a very serious incident— there are few small bulk chemical or oil product claims; when they arise they are usually very large indeed.

Insufficient statistical data is available to explain how most of these contamination claims arise. However, it is suggested that there are two major causes:

(i) inadequate preparation/cleaning of the cargo carrying compartment and/or pipelines or

(ii) a 'human error' in wrongly manipulating valves etc.

Certainly claims arising from (i) should not arise and should be capable of prevention. Claims arising from (ii) probably cannot be eradicated completely, but could possibly be reduced considerably by ensuring that personnel controlling the movement of cargo are properly qualified, experienced and know their own ship intimately!

Of course, it is possible that the cargo is contaminated before it is actually loaded on board. Liquid cargo samples should be drawn from the manifold and analysed if appropriate.

Dry bulk cargoes should be exmained for any obvious contamination and any problems should be dealt with there and then and an appropriate remark entered on the bill of lading, where necessary.

2.6.4. Condensation/sweat damage claims

Condensation claims are significant, as will be seen from figure 6. Because of the nature of sea transport, it may be inevitable that condensation damage will occur to the cargo—for example the vessel may encounter very heavy weather and the ventilation system may have to be shut down for a number of days to prevent sea water which is being taken on deck, entering the cargo compartments via the ventilation system. Under such circumstances if condensation did occur and cargo was damaged as a result, then the shipowner should be able to successfully repudiate liability on the basis of a peril of the seas defence. However, to do so the shipowner would need to produce all the relevant evidence—e.g. hold temperature, dew point and ventilation records, accurate details of the heavy weather experienced from independent sources as well as the ship's own log books etc. Without such evidence it would be very difficult to successfully defeat a condensation damage claim in its entirety.

However, condensation damage claims have often arisen because the cargo was ventilated at the wrong time, or was not ventilated when necessary. The determining factors are temperature and dew point. Invariably, upon investigation, it transpires that the responsible officer had not carried out the ventilation along scientific or good seamanship lines, but rather he ventilated every day when the sun was shining! Most of these claims could have been avoided/ prevented if greater care had been taken with the ventilation. Accordingly, the shipowner should ensure that the ventilation requirements of a particular cargo on a particular voyage are fully understood by the Master, prior to leaving the loading port and that the Master is under instruction to keep the relevant records and to ventilate only when appropriate. If this is done, then claims are unlikely to arise.

2.6.5. Handling damage

Damages due to bad handling are clearly more likely to be significant with reefer, containerised and general cargoes as well as specific types of commodities such as steel and bagged cargoes. This is apparent from diagram 7 and suggested in figure 6, although a number of categories of damage seem to be linked together under 'physical'.

This is a very significant head of claim and will invariably be the direct result of bad practices by stevedores.

Such bad practices range from the use of 'cargo hooks' or 'pad eyes' to manoeuvre bagged cargo causing tearing damage and spillage of the cargo, to using a totally inadequate lifting device when loading containers, carrying possibly 20 tonnes of cargo, so that one container crashes on to another full of valuable cargo—see figure 9 (page 50).

Since most of these handling damage claims are caused by bad practices, it must surely be possible to reduce the damage considerably by adopting good systems

Hopefully, rational persuasion may work, but if the stevedores are being paid on a 'piece rate' basis then their priorities may lie elsewhere. Another tactic which should be adopted is to carefully record what damage the stevedores are doing—while trying one's very best to persuade them to change their bad practices—and then pursue an action against them for an indemnity for the claim brought by the cargo owners against the shipowners. The Master should recognise his responsibilities under the Hague Rules to care for the cargo in his custody, and the obligation he has to the cargo owner to carefully handle the cargo so that the cargo owner may expect to receive the cargo in the same good order and condition it was in when loaded. The Master should cease loading until an acceptable method of loading the cargo is adopted. Clearly, the Master will not be the most popular person in the port, having done this. In some countries he may not get away with it, charterers may threaten to put the vessel off-hire, amongst other things. However, if the Master has acted reasonably, and if a dispute ensues and is pursued, then the writer would feel reasonably confident that commercial arbitrators or judges would back up the Master's decision. Please remember, though, that good evidence is vital. It is hoped that charterers and/or shippers will accept that the Master is in the right and will take the necessary steps to ensure that the stevedores adopt good handling practices. Photographs provide invaluable evidence for this purpose.

2.6.6. Off-spec. cargoes

The problem of 'off-spec.' cargo does not seem to be covered by the UK Club statistical diagrams, but 'pre-shipment quality' is possibly one and the same thing.

The issue was touched on at the end of section 2.6.3. above, that the cargo could be 'off-spec.' or contaminated, or otherwise not in perfect condition prior to it being delivered to the vessel. The important point to remember is that the Master is not expected to be an analytical chemist. He is expected, though, to carry out a reasonable inspection of the cargo at the time of loading and, if appropriate, either refuse to load the cargo or to enter a suitable remark on the bill of lading. It is a good practice to draw joint samples of liquid cargoes at the ship's manifold for sampling purposes.

If the claim is for 'off-spec.' cargo or relating to 'pre-shipment quality', and provided the 'reasonable' steps were taken by those on board, then the claim would lie between the buyer and the seller under the sale contract, rather than under the contract of carriage.

2.6.7. Inadequate stowage

This is closely linked with the handling type damage discussed in 2.6.5. above. Indeed, many of the issues involved are identical. In figure 6 this category is probably lumped in with bad handling, and considered 'physical' (damage) but in figure 7 it is separated out and is clearly the single biggest cause of cargo claims.

The types of claims arising under this category have probably resulted from the stow collapsing or shifting due to inadequate securing, or unseamanlike practices in stowing the cargo. Most of these claims could have been avoided.

A frequent scenario is where a bulk carrier is time chartered into a liner type service for which she is totally unsuitable. The charterers attempt to load containers without any securing devices, just piled on top of each other with very little, if any, lashing or securing. As soon as the ship encounters even moderate weather conditions the inevitable happens and the stow collapses. The shipowner is usually left to solve the problem. Photographs 10 to 13 (pages 50 and 52) depict the typical consequences of inadequate stowage.

Unfortunately there is something of a 'grey' area; regarding the Master's responsibility for the stowage of cargo under certain time charter parties. Clearly, under a contract of carriage evidenced by a bill of lading which incorporates the Hague Rules, the Master has a responsibility towards cargo interests to '. . . properly and carefully load, handle, stow. etc . . . the goods carried . . .' (Art III Rule 2) Therefore he must protect the cargo interests' position and ensure that the stow is such that the cargo will not shift or collapse or suffer some other fate during the voyage. Under the governing time charter party it may be clear that (for example Clause 8 of the N.Y.P.E. charter party)—'. . . the captain (although appointed by the owners), shall be under the orders and directions of the charterers as regards employment and agency; and charterers are to load, stow, and trim the cargo at their expense under the supervision of the captain . . .'. The question is what does the term 'supervision' actually mean? The charterers are clearly the ones carrying out the job of loading the cargo and they will be legally liable for the consequences of their action—the responsibility would not shift on to the Master because of his 'supervisory' role.

In fact the English courts have dealt with the question and, very simply, the Master's supervisory role is limited to ensuring that his vessel remains seaworthy at all stages of loading and that includes ensuring that the cargo is stowed and secured in such a way that it will not shift or collapse to such an extent that it could affect the seaworthiness of his ship.

What is not clear though, as far as the writer is aware, is the position where the charterers are insisting on a method of stowage which is bad and will cause damage to the cargo but will not affect the seaworthiness of the vessel. On the face of it the Master would be obliged to comply with the orders of the charterers under the charter party but this could compromise his position *vis-à-vis* his responsibilities under the contract evidenced by the bill of lading.

2.6.8. Unsuitable vessels

It would appear from figure 7 that claims arising from the unsuitability of vessels are at the lower end of the scale. The writer would suggest that this is probably as a result of interpretation in identifying the proximate cause of the loss or damage. As was suggested in section 2.6.7., many of the cargo damage claims which have been categorised as having occurred due to 'bad stowage' were probably a result of the particular vessel being unsuitable for the carriage of that particular cargo. For example containers loaded in the holds of a bulk carrier may well have collapsed because they had not been stowed and secured adequately, but the reason they could not be adequately secured was because the bulk carrier was not designed or fitted for the carriage of containers—one could say the real cause was the unsuitability of the vessel.

The point is that almost all of these claims could have been avoided. A vessel chartered into a service to carry containers should be properly fitted with container stacking shoes, and suitable and sufficient lashing points, the cargo should be lashed and secured in such a way that it will not collapse or shift when the vessel meets heavy weather. The bottom line, apparently, is money—the cost of additional lashings and time for the charterers, or the financial consequences of cargo damage claims which will often fall on the shipowners. What must never be compromised, though, is the seaworthiness of the vessel—including the stowage and securing of the cargo.

3.0.0. Why have these claims arisen?

This is an obvious and important question to ask but as has already been suggested the answer is far from straight forward. Indeed it would be correct to say that there is no clear all encompassing answer available. There are many factors which need to be taken into account before an answer can even be attempted.

3.1.0. No single cause

Figure 14 (page 49), reproduced from the *UK P&I Club Analysis of Major Claims 1992* shows the main cause of all major claims as a percentage of the total number of claims. The lower section of the diagram shows the actual number of incidents ascribed to a particular cause.

This diagram clearly shows that there is no single cause of these claims.

The validity of the UK P&I Club's figures was confirmed by a similar analysis recently carried out by another large P&I Club—the West of England—and the results of their analysis are shown in figure 15 (page 49) which is reproduced from the *West of England Annual Review 1992*.

One identifiable cause which immediately stands out in the results of these analyses is the very high percentage attributable to human error in one form or another. This will be discussed in much more detail in sections 3.5.ff.

Within the context of this paper on cargo claims, the UK P&I report has produced a diagram showing the distribution of all cargo claims by main cause—see figure 16 (page 53). It can be seen that almost half the claims appear to be caused by human error; 40% are caused by ship failures and the remainder are still under investigation.

3.2.0. Physical condition of the ship

It can be seen from figure 7 that defective hatch covers represents the second single largest cause of claims by number and shell plate failure accounted for the highest single value of claim. Valve/pipe failure, inadequate hold/tank cleaning and ship machinery failure also figure significantly. Other factors linked with the condition of the ship are also identified such as blocked bilges, inadequate tank coatings, bulkhead failure, leaking double bottoms and main engine failure.

Horrific sights have been seen in recent years of large sections of shell plating literally falling off the side of the ship or the entire bow section falling off.

Much more frequently it is found that cargo has been severely damaged because of seriously defective hatch covers—mostly patent steel hatch covers.

The answer to the immediate question why the shell plating or bow section fell off or why the hatch covers leaked is probably fairly simple—they had been inadequately maintained. When the next question is asked 'Why were they inadequately maintained?' the answer is probably because of economic reasons. The question which really needs to be asked is how these ships, the vast majority of them fully classed, were allowed to fall into such decrepid states without detection by the regulatory bodies.

It was as a direct result of the repeated incidence of cargo damage resulting from inadequate maintenance that most of the P&I Clubs introduced their own condition surveys on certain vessels utilising independent surveyors. Certain Hull and Machinery underwriters have, more recently, followed suit and were horrified to find that out of every ten ships chosen at random, all of which were in class, maybe eight failed to achieve the prescribed standards.

Major charterers are also heavily involved these days carrying out their own condition surveys before agreeing to take the relevant vessel on charter.

3.2.1. Age of the ship

It may appear to be an obvious inference to draw that the physical condition of the ship, and the claims which have been linked to the physical condition of the ship, are directly related to the age of the ship.

The fact is that the older ship which has been well maintained, with a motivated crew on board and good management ashore can run almost claim free. Whereas a newer ship, with inadequate maintenance, poorly motivated crew and poor management ashore is very likely to have serious cargo claims.

This observation is perhaps supported by the UK P&I Club's analysis—see figure 17 (page 61). This series of diagrams shows the distribution of claims by age band, for each type of ship involved. The table compares this with the distribution, by age band, of entered ships of each type. For each kind of ship the table highlights, as a possible risk indicator, the age bands for which the claims profile shows a higher incidence than the profile of the UK Club's entry.

It can be seen that 25% of the UK Club's reefer ships are aged 5-9 years old, but they were involved in 35% of the major reefer claims. For container ships the two profiles match within a reasonable margin of error. For tankers 40% of their major claims arise on ships aged 15-19 years, but these make up only 20% of the tankers entered in that Association. There is a similar pattern for bulk carriers, with 15-19 year old ships comprising only 21% of the entry, but bringing in 35% of the claims. Amongst dry cargo ships, it is the 10-14 year olds which are the culprits, with 26% of the dry cargo ship entry incurring 35% of the claims.

A further interesting set of comparative statistics was produced by the Britannia Steamship Insurance Association Ltd in their *Britannia News* No. 17 of July 1992, which compared the percentage of claims, by number of that club, above 150,000 with the percentage of ships entered in the club with the percentage of ships in the World Fleet. These statistics are reproduced in figure 18 (page 53).

3.2.2. Lack of maintenance

The problems and consequences of lack of maintenance were touched upon in section 3.2.0. above.

A chord was struck in 1992 when the House of Lords Select Committee on Science and Technology issued its report on the *Safety Aspects of Ship Design and Technology*. In that report, at section 2.2.0., their Lordships drew attention to a new type of shipowner '. . . the bean counter'. The text states '. . . he (the bean counter) is not committed to his ships or their masters, but manages his fleet at arm's length through ship management companies and manning agencies. Even when the management company is a responsible one, the resulting length, complexity and weakness of the management chain militate against good safety management . . .'.

The bean counter is interested only in short-term profit. He sees safety-related expenditure, such as maintenance or training, as cost rather than investment . . . , and casualties not as something to avoid but something to insure against . . . . We suggest that shipping has always had its 'bean counters', but

we are prepared to believe that they control a more significant slice of world shipping than they used to . . . .

It certainly is possible, in the short term, to save money by cutting back on essential maintenance but at what cost? Not only in respect of substantially increased insurance costs—see figure 4—but all too often in seafarers' lives.

3.3.0 Depressed market

It is fairly well recognised that the market conditions in shipping are cyclical and are driven by that most basic of economics laws 'supply and demand'. Unfortunately it would seem that the present depressed part of the cycle is lasting very much longer than previously.

Freight rates and charter hire rates are far too low in most markets. The cost of a new building is too high and cannot even be contemplated in most cases.

In an attempt to make ends meet some shipowners have no doubt been tempted to reduce their running costs by various means; 'flagging out', employing cheaper crews, cutting back on maintenance etc. and the consequences have already been seen—substantially higher insurance costs.

Certainly the shipowner can be criticised for many of the steps taken for economic reasons but they are not all 'bean counters'. Many shipowners would like nothing more than to be able to afford a highly motivated, experienced and qualified crew; to keep their vessels in a first class standard as far as maintenance and equipment is concerned; to replace the older tonnage with new buildings but the reality is that they do not have bottomless pockets.

To allow shipowners to achieve such goals there must be an increase in the charter hire and freight rates. Clearly if cargo shippers and charterers were to pay more for the cost of transporting goods by sea then this must be passed on to the end user of the goods—the final purchaser/consumer.

The question would seem to be therefore 'for how long can the shipowners of the world continue to subsidise the end user/consumer of cargoes which are carried by sea?'.

3.4.0. The United States disease

There has developed a phenomena during the last few years which has become known as the 'United States Disease'; and this disease appears to be contagious.

The symptoms of this disease are very large claims against shipowners, and their insurers, with frequently little supporting evidence. The most blatant manifestation of this phenomena is in the realm of personal injury claims where allegedly injured stevedores, for example, pursue claims for many millions of dollars. To a lesser extent it has also been seen in cargo claims and it appears in many cases that claims for alleged damage to steel cargo, for example, seem to have been formulated even before the vessel arrives at her discharge port!

Many Third World countries, in particular, have been quick to seize upon the opportunity of a foreign ship bringing in cargo to lodge claims and impose customs fines to generate a lucrative source of foreign currency. Indeed the UK Club report states that 'only 8% by number of major cargo claims arise in Africa but they account for 23% of the value'.

Figure 19 (page 53), reproduced for the UK Club report, compares the countries in which the incidents occurred with the jurisdictions in which the claims are pursued. Although the UK is the country of incident for less than 4% of the claims as measured by number or by value, it is nevertheless the jurisdiction in which 15%, by number, and 27%, by value, of the claims are pursued. The UK Club suggests that this is a reflection not only of the frequency with which carriage contracts provide for UK jurisdiction, but also of the prominence of London insurance markets. In any event, the very high average value (almost $700,000) of claims pursued in the UK puts into perspective the idea that forum shoppers generally have the United States at the top of their list.

3.5.0. Human element

Early in 1991 the Maritime Directorate of the UK Department of Transport issued a report *The Human Element in Shipping Casualties*. Recognising the aversion of many to reading detailed technical reports the Maritime Directorate published a summary report based on the research carried out by the Tavistock Institute of Human Relations. This is a most readable and illuminating document.

In paragraph 1/17 of the Marine Directorate report attention is drawn to a statistic: '. . . 80 to 90% of all accidents are caused by human error . . .'. The report suggests, however, with reference to marine casualties '. . . it is more accurate to say that human involvement (often associated with other factors) is found in a very high proportion of those cases where a judgement can be made consistent with the available data . . .'.

We should indeed excercise some caution when we use the expression 'human error'—it can mean different things to different people. In the claims review section of the *Britannia News* attention is correctly drawn to the necessity to be quite clear about what we mean by 'human error'. The review points out that '. . . it is freely applied by most people, for instance, both to acts of simple mistake and to acts of gross negligence'. Yet these are two very different types of 'error' which ought to be distinguished . . . . The writer would fully concur with that observation.

In February 1992, the House of Lords Select Committee on Science and Technology issued its report on the Safety Aspects of Ship Design & Technology! In discussing the Human Element, in paragraph 4.2, the report states '. . . it is received wisdom that four out of five ship casualties—80% —are due to "human error".

This convenient statistic should be handled with care. Firstly, most ship casualties have a multiplicity of related causes, and attempts to nominate a single or principal cause will in many cases involve violence to the facts. One reason for wishing to assign a cause to a casualty is in order to determine whether it is covered by insurance . . . secondly, whose errors are counted? The Salvage Association reckoned that of all the causes in their tabulation the ones which could not involve 'human error' were war, hurricane/typhoon, latent defect and design fault; yet casualty through war or weather may be blamed on the master or owner who put the ship in the danger zone, and the other two causes involve, respectively, errors by the manufacturer and the designer, who are human too! Following this line of reasoning some witnesses suggested that a truer figure for the proportion of accidents due to human error would be 100% . . . .

According to the *UK Club Analysis of Major Claims:* 'Human error was the main cause of half the cargo claims, half the pollution claims, 65% of the personal injuries, 80% of the property damage, and 90% of the collisions'.

Figures 14 (page 49) and 16 (page 53) provide a clear indication of the significance of 'human error' in the overall claims experience.

In their *Analysis of Major Claims* the UK Club also explores the philosophical analysis of what is meant by the term error! They suggest that it is '. . . used here somewhat loosely to encompass any human action or omission identifiable as the immediate cause of the event from which the liability arises. So defined, a wide range of more or less blameworthy behaviour, from simple mistake in arithmetic, through errors in judgement, to deliberate risk taking is included . . .'.

They continue the analysis of the concept 'error' by suggesting that, in this wide sense it has many sources: '. . . it may arise from a lack of knowledge or experience. On the other hand, even well-informed and properly trained personnel can become over-confident, careless, or even reckless in responding to commercial pressures. Then there are temperamental factors such as fatigue, discomfort, boredom, anger, unhappiness, illness, or confusion, which all make people more prone to mistakes than might otherwise be the case . . .'.

They continue to discuss a number of specific examples but conclude by conceding: '. . . such forms of human error, to the extent that they arise from the natural distractions of human temperament and mood are, by their very nature not possible to completely eliminate. At best, well designed working environment and procedures can help to reduce them'.

The UK Club also produces a most interesting statistic reproduced at figure 20 (page 61). In this diagram the major claims caused by human error (about 860) are distributed by age band of the ships involved, together with a similar distribution for major claims caused by ship failure (about 450) and for the entry of all ships in the UK Club. They point out that ship failures (i.e. claims caused by structural failure, mechanical failure, or equipment failure) peak in ships aged 10-14 years, then decline somewhat in ships aged 15-19 thereafter dropping sharply. Human errors rise in ships aged 5-9 years but they too peak in ships aged 10-14 years and thereafter decline.

In their report the UK Club raises the question: 'Why is it that both human errors and ship failures peak in the 10-14 year old ships?'

In answer to this question they suggest: '. . . There is no doubt that age is causally relevant to ship failure, given the correlation of risk factors, it seems reasonable to suggest that the difficulties of running ships which are beginning to fail may account in turn for the high incidence of human error amongst those who work such ships . . . '.

The UK Club concludes that the table, figure 21 lends some support to the views of those who think it possible that a good many human errors might have been avoidable had the ships involved been maintained to a higher standard.

The writer has not had access to the UK Club's data against which it produced the analysis report. However, he could venture to speculate that if the so called 'ship failure' incidents were reduced by one further stage then 'human error' would also be identified as the primary cause. This would resolve the apparent dichotomy and suggest that the related problems are closer than they may at first have appeared.

Figure 21 (page 64), reproduced from the *UK Club Analysis of Major Claims*, compares the number of claims caused by ship failure against the number of claims caused by human error.

3.5.1. Simple mistake/error of judgement

In the last section, mention was made of the important distinction which must be made between acts of simple mistake and to acts of gross negligence—both of which can be described as 'human error'.)

Britannia in their article clarify the distinction by the use of an example:

'If a Master approaching a familiar dock, without the assistance of a pilot, slightly misjudges the strength of the wind and tide causing the ship to damage the dock, most would accuse him of an unfortunate error of judgement, no more. If, on the other hand, a ship loses its deck cargo of lumber because, for fear of missing the next fixture, the Master refused to reduce speed in poor weather, "gross negligence" might appear more accurate.'

As Britannia point out, the distinction is important for two reasons: '. . . Firstly, little can be done to eradicate errors of judgement or simple mistakes. They happen to all of us and probably always will. On the other hand, it is hoped that much can be done to eradicate incompetence and negligence. Secondly, "human error" is rather too comfortable and vague an expression which can be used, precisely because of its lack of definition to obscure and excuse poor standards and (occasionally) extreme incompetence . . . '

In the next ten short sections, some of the more common contributory causes of human error will be examined in a little more detail.

3.5.2.0. Incompetence/negligence

Incompetence and negligence can arise either as a result of lack of training or lack of experience. Each of these factors in itself is a very serious potential risk factor for accidents and claims, but often the two factors are combined where the relevant personnel have neither the training nor the practical experience to carry out their jobs efficiently. The accidents and claims are just waiting to happen.

It is difficult to comprehend how some shipowners and shipmanagers can adopt such relaxed attitudes to the standards of training and experience of their master, officer and crew. These people are being placed on board a ship which is possibly worth many millions of dollars, to transport a cargo worth many more millions of dollars and during this time is exposed to numerous third party liabilities, some of which could, potentially, run into hundreds of millions of dollars. Logic would dictate that the most careful scrutiny should be carried out in selecting people of the highest standards to be trusted with such valuable assets. In reality many crews, from the master downwards, are recruited through manning agents in third world countries, little checking seems to be done into the actual qualifications and experience of individuals and rarely have the same crew sailed together previously.

3.5.2.1. As a result of inadequate basic education/training

Whilst there have been attempts to standardise the education and training of ships' officers around the world— the most notable attempt being the IMO promulgated STCW Convention— this does not appear to have produced uniform standards.

In most of the traditional maritime nations there have been fewer and fewer cadets trained during the last decade or so and it is extremely difficult to persuade the right calibre of person to even consider a seagoing career. This places even greater demand on the labour force of certain third world countries. Without doubt there are some very well trained and experienced seafarers available from these labour pools but there are also many who simply have not undergone sufficient basic training before being given their Certificates of Competency and, with it, a responsible position on board ship.

In any event, as far as the main subject of this paper is concerned, i.e. cargo claims and loss prevention, it is important to note that neither the STCW Convention nor the syllabus of any maritime nation concentrates upon, in any detail, the very function of the Merchant Marine i.e. to carry cargoes from 'A' to 'B'. Certainly the important safety subjects of navigation, stability, seamanship etc. are all covered, and so they should be, but the commercial, legal and insurance subjects are only superficially looked at.

Claims avoidance does not seem to figure significantly; in a recent piece of research of nautical training establishments around the world which the writer carried out— *The Human Element in Claims—What Role for the P&I Clubs?* — more than 80% of the nautical training establishments participating felt that more time should be spent on commercial subjects—but not at the expense of the important safety subjects. More than half the colleges stated that they considered the existing syllabus inadequate in the area of commercial, legal and insurance subjects and it does not adequately equip the master/officer to deal with commercial problems on board ship.

3.5.2.2. As a result of inexperience

There is truth in the old cliche that there is 'no substitute for experience'. It is certainly possible to train a reasonably intelligent individual to pass an examination of a master in a fairly short period of time but few officers with a newly acquired master's ticket, for example, would have sufficient practical 'hands on' experience effectively and adequately to take command of an ocean-going vessel. The reality is though that there is such a shortage of properly certificated officers around the world—and the situation is going to get worse—that the watch keeping officer, and indeed masters have frequently very little 'seatime' under their belt, but their possession of the relevant certificates satisfies the appropriate flag State manning regulations, the port State control regulations and insurance requirements.

It is a supply and demand situation but an inexperienced master, officers and crew must pose a substantially greater risk of having accidents and being involved in claim incidents than a master, officers and crew with the sort of operating experience that existed amongst the traditional maritime nations a few years ago.

3.5.3.0. Multi/cross cultural issues

For many years there have existed ships with mixed nationalities e.g. European Master and officers with Indian sailors, which ran very well indeed.

However, there seems to be a growing trend, over the last few years, to put together a crew of many nationalities with little thought being applied to how they may perform as a team. This is a formula for disaster!

A number of related issues will be considered in this subsection; to some extent these are sociological issues.

3.5.3.1. Languages

There have been a number of major incidents during the last few years which have been exacerbated, if not caused, by a breakdown of communication through the inability of two or more key players to speak in a common language.

There have been many more minor incidents where this has been a serious and significant issue. An example of one incident which was reported to the writer by a P&I correspondent was where the Master of a ship could only speak to the officer of the watch—a third mate—through an interpreter. Clearly, the propensity for accidents to happen—as a result of confusion—is less likely if everyone speaks and understands a common language. The international language in shipping, like it or not, is English. Where multilingual crews are employed then it is imperative that they speak this common language.

Also, within the context of cargo claims, it is important that the various documents; bills of lading, manifest, charter parties, cargo carrying instructions are also prepared in a language understood by those on board, ideally in English. If they are not then the Master should seek help and should not sign any document which he is not able to read and understand.

3.5.3.2. Cultural compatibility

Crews of a single nationality and/or culture can often work very well together with an harmonious attitude. However, deeply rooted tensions or simply lack of understanding of the other's position can quickly lead to conflict, at worst, and apathetic indifference at best, when people of different nationalities and/or cultures are placed in the restricted confines of a shipboard existence.

These tensions and conflicts lead not only to a disharmonious attitude on board but also an unsafe working environment. People are more concerned with the developing acrimony than with the maintenance of the ship and caring for the cargo.

Within the small confines of a ship's complement there needs to be a good working relationship. This is built on trust and mutual respect and understanding. If due regard is not given to cultural compatibility, then such trust and respect will never develop and it is more likely to degenerate into something quite the opposite. This will create a negative attitude towards the important job of running the ship and the general safety.

3.5.4.0. Motivational issues

It would be difficult to draw a line between some of the sociological issues raised previously and the psychological issues raised in relation to motivation.

Common sense, if nothing else, would dictate that if the seafarers on board a ship, from the Master down, were highly motivated then their approach to their job would be conscientious and dedicated. They would naturally give their best to the successful running of the ship and, consequently, the number of accidents and claims would very likely be much reduced.

The questions which need to be asked, therefore, are:

(a) Is there a motivational problem?

(b) If so, why?

(c) What, if anything, can be done to overcome the problem?

The answer to the first question, it is suggested is 'yes and no'. The indications are that if due regard has been given to the make up of nationalities and cultures of the crew, where there is some form of continuity of employment, where the financial remunerations are adequate, where there is good professional management of the ship, both ashore and afloat, then motivation tends to be high. Unfortunately, in the depressed shipping market of today such instances are very rare—some would perhaps doubt their very existence!

For many seafarers today, of whatever nationality, they are at sea because it is the most lucrative job they can get; the aim is to earn as much money as possible in as short a period of time as possible. Any motivation which exists seems to be directed towards personal goals rather than the success of the maritime adventure.

3.5.4.1. Casual labour

This malaise is probably best epitomised in the growing tendency to employ what can perhaps be described as casual labour. A shipowner may put his ships out to management; the ship management company may sub-contract with a manning agency. The crew who are provided, from the Master downwards, may never have sailed with each other before, they may be of different nationalities and

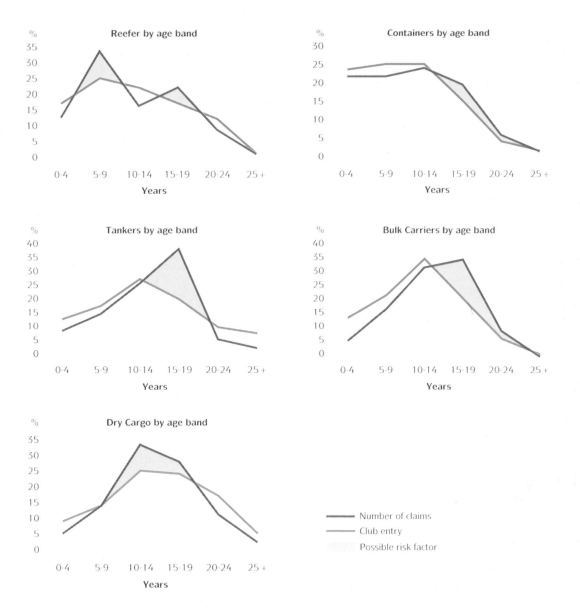

Fig 17: Distribution by age band for five types of ship, compared with Club entry (UK Club 1992).

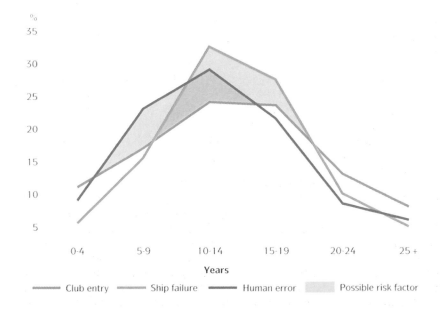

Fig 20: Distribution by ship age band of all (863) human error claims; and distribution by age band of all (451) ship failure claims, compared with Club entry (UK Club 1992).

incompatible cultures, they may never have sailed with the particular ship or shipping or management company before and at the end of their term of employment may never sail together or with that same company again.

There is no sense of belonging to each other or to the shipping or management company. Any loyalty which may exist is more likely to be to the manning agents.

Under such circumstances there is little or no interest or indeed incentive to work towards a profitable claim-free voyage. Such crews often feel exploited by their employers and find that they have to live in poor conditions on board. Whilst this is a bleak picture which is being painted, it is not universal, but it is encountered with sufficient frequency, as attested by such bodies as the ITF and the Missions to Seamen, to suggest that there is a serious problem. Who can really expect such a crew to be highly motivated?

The lack of motivation, lack of interest and lack of commitment will inevitably lead to lower standards all round, which, in turn, will lead to accidents and claims.

3.5.4.2. Discontinuity of employment

It is suggested that the key problem, and possibly the solution, lies in the question of continuity of employment

There was a time, not so long go, when the Master, officers and many of the crew were employed by a shipping company, possibly on a company contract, and many would have spent their entire seagoing career with that one company. There was a great loyalty of the employee towards his employer and vice versa. There was a strong feeling of 'we'; a sense of belonging. It was not unusual for the same crew to be assigned to the same ship for a number of years. Yes, money was important on a personal level, but there was also a pride in one's own professionalism, in one's ship and in the company. These ingredients produced a strong motivating factor to ensure that the ship ran well, that she was well maintained and that the voyage ran smoothly and there was a sense of achievement when the voyage was satisfactorily completed and the cargo discharged without loss or damage.

With the loss of that continuity of employment which took place towards the end of the 1970s, the motivational ingredients were also lost.

It is the writer's personal belief that unless and until that recipe is restored then little will be achieved to encourage a more claims conscious attitude on board or to implement, in a meaningful way, any loss prevention measures.

3.6.0. The unavoidable accident

Almost two thousand years ago, the Roman historian, Livy, wrote the following canny lines:

'To err is human; indeed, it is the cause of most of our misery. Invariably, though, it is to the gods that we look for remedy'

In the *Britannia News Claims Review* they wittily add the post script:

'Today, few look to the gods for assistance when things go wrong, most turn to their insurers instead.'

It would be very naive to believe that all accidents could be prevented or that human error could be overcome completely. Human beings are fallible and they will err. However, there is little doubt that much can be done to reduce the number and size of claims resulting from human error.

There are certain categories of incidents though which could be said as accidents, for example, so called Acts of God, Perils of the Sea, Acts of War, Inherent Vice etc. These will all be examined in the next four sections.

3.6.1. Act of God—perils of the seas

Acts of God and perils of the seas tend to be lumped together and, under the Hague Rules, tend to be generally referred to as the heavy weather defences.

This is in recognition that the carriage of goods by sea can mean that the ship and cargo can be exposed to extraordinary events over which the shipowner has no control and, consequently, will not be considered to blame if damage occurs.

Acts of God may include such things as tidal waves, volcanic disturbances, lightening, earthquakes. Where a shipowner attempts to raise this as a defence to avoid liability in circumstances where a loss occurs from such an inevitable accident, he must discharge his primary obligations under Article III Rule 1 before reliance may be placed on the defence.

On the face of it the defence of '. . . perils, dangers and accidents of the sea or other navigable waters . . . ' Hague Rules— Article IV Rule 2 (c) would seem to be very wide; however, in practice the Courts tend to construe the exception as striclty as possible so as to restrict the shipowners' ability to rely on them.

If a shipowner is attempting to run a 'heavy weather defence' it is usually because the cargo has been damaged either:

(a) by an ingress of seawater;

(b) by a shift of stow;

(c) by condensation.

Before the shipowner can attempt such a defence under (a) he would have to demonstrate that the ingress did not occur as a result of any fault on his part to exercise due diligence to make the vessel seaworthy. This is a very difficult burden to overcome. He would also have to demonstrate that the weather was more severe than could be reasonably expected at that time of year in that geographical position—i.e. the weather conditions were unexpected and extraordinary.

Similar tests would apply before the shipowner could attempt to raise a defence under (b). In addition, he would also have to demonstrate that the cargo was adequately secured at the commencement of the voyage. The presumption is that if it had been adequately secured then it should not have shifted— since it did shift it probably wasn't adequately secured in the first place! It is a very difficult argument to overcome.

Example (c) is probably the incident where the shipowner is likely to stand most chance of successfully raising a defence. This is where the ventilation system has had to be closed down during heavy weather—to prevent sea water entering the cargo compartments via the ventilators—and sweat damage occurs. However, to successfully run such a defence it would be imperative to be able to demonstrate, from well maintained contemporaneous documentation, what the weather was like, when ventilation was carried out, when it was suspended etc. Accordingly, ventilation records, hold temperature and dew-point records should be kept as well as an accurate record of the weather in the log book. These records should not only be kept during periods of heavy weather but should be maintained during the normal course of the voyage as a matter of routine and good seamanship.

3.6.2. Act of war etc.

Act of war, act of public enemies, arrest or restraint of Princes, rulers of people or seizure under legal process are all defences available to a shipowner under he Hague Rules, although they are rarely invoked.

These exceptions probably only apply to recognised states of war or hostilities between States or forcible interference by governments or sovereign powers. The question of whether the damage to the cargo was an 'unavoidable accident' will depend upon the circumstances of the case. Why was the ship where she was when the damage occurred?

3.6.3. Inherent Vice

Although the defence is usually generally referred to as 'Inherent Vice' it is worth noting that Hague Rules—Article IV Rule 2 (m) actually says: '. . . wastage in bulk or weight or any other loss or damage arising from inherent defect, quality, or vice of the goods'.

It may well be that certain products or commodities do have the propensity to self-heat or even ignite or lose weight or some other detrimental quality, and this may be well known. However, if cargo is lost or damaged and the shipowner attempts to raise a defence of 'inherent vice' he must be able to demonstrate that he took all reasonable precautions and, particularly, that he properly and carefully loaded, handled, stowed, carried, kept and cared for the goods as required under Hague Rules Article III Rule 2. Not only that, but he must also be able to demonstrate the deficiencies in the cargo were not apparent at the time of loading.

Whether or not the shipowner can rely on an Inherent Vice defence and claim that the damage was as a result of an unavoidable accident will depend, very much, on the circumstances of the particular case.

4.0.0. What can be done to prevent claims arising?

There is a basic presumption which we must make if we are to attempt to reduce the number and size of cargo claims and that is that there is something that can be done to prevent these claims arising!

As has already been stated; there is rarely one single cause attributable to any individual accident, incident or claim, but rather there tend to be a multitude of factors. This section will examine some of the more significant factors and will suggest some solutions.

4.1.0. Policing the physical condition of the ships

It is well known that the average age of the world fleet is increasing. Ships which should have gone for scrap are continuing trading 'for a few more years' and few shipowners are in a position to purchase new buildings. With the depressed shipping market which has been experienced over the last decade or so maintenance budgets have been cut. With reduced numbers of crew, poorly motivated crew and rapid turn around in port an on-going maintenance programme may have been more and more difficult to maintain.

It has already been shown in Section 3.2.0.ff that the physical condition and age of the vessel can have a significant bearing on the likelihood of the vessel being involved in a major claim. The question needs to be asked; how and why are there so many sub-standard ships still sailing the oceans? What is being done to check up on them and what may be the consequences of discovering such vessels?

4.1.1. Classification societies

Reduced to its simplest form, the role of the classification society was, and should be, to provide some form of independent warranty to the shipowners' and cargo owners' insurers that the ship is sound and 'a good risk'. Historically that was the very reason why classification societies were founded. This worked well for many years but during the last decade or so may classification societies have bowed to pressure from a number of shipowners to reduce their standards. As a consequence, many insurers, both hull and machinery and P&I Clubs, can no longer rely upon classification society surveys to confirm that the vessel is likely to be a 'good risk'. There are too many documented cases of ships being found in very serious states of disrepair having recently been issued with appropriate classification certificates. In extreme cases there are incidents of entire bow sections or large pieces of shell plating literally falling off with classification certificates only a couple of months old.

The writer handled a case just a few years ago where a ship was issued with an interim certificate of class by a very well known classification society in one port. She sailed to her port of loading where she loaded a full cargo of bagged sugar. During the voyage she experienced heavy weather, about force 8. Every hatch cover leaked; bunker oil, fresh water and ballast water all leaked into the cargo compartments. The entire cargo was a total loss.

It is suggested that there is a fundamental flaw in the system of classification societies. There is an old expression that 'he who pays the piper calls the tune'. At the moment the one who pays the piper, and thus calls the tune, is the shipowner. The threats made to the classification societies by some shipowners is to the effect that if they do not issue the classification certificate as required by the shipowner then the ship will be moved to a classification society who will be more accommodating.

Fig 21: Comparison of human error and ship failure by age band for five types of ship (source UK Club analysis of major claims 1992).

Fig 22: It is important to reject damaged cargo.

During very recent years, most of the reputable societies have made serious attempts to overcome such threats by joining the International Association of Classification Societies (IACS) to set down minimum standards to which all members will comply and to ensure that if a vessel entered in one IACS society fails to meet those standards then she will not be accepted by another member. This is clearly a very positive move forward and deserves to be supported.

Another positive step which could be taken, perhaps, is for the insurer to be the one who 'pays the piper' and thus 'calls the tune'. The shipowner would still be paying in the long run, through his insurance premium or 'call', but this would surely remove the 'commercial' pressure which some shipowners still try to exert upon their classification societies. The original purpose of the societies could then be fully restored. It would also remove the necessity for the duplication of surveys which now takes place by most of the P&I Clubs and an increasing number of hull and machinery underwriters.

4.1.2. P&I condition surveys

All the P&I Clubs of the International Group carry out condition surveys of one description or another on vessels entered in their club or on vessels which are offered for entry. However, different clubs have very different standards, procedures and requirements! Some clubs limit their condition surveys to vessels over, say, 12 years of age being offered to the club. Other clubs have a much more sophisticated arrangement with a sizeable in-house staff of ship inspectors. These inspectors may be located in a certain port and will visit ships entered with that club during a stay in that port. He will have a general look at the overall condition of the ship and meet the Master and other officers. Drawing upon their own vast experience the club's ship inspector will form a general impression of the ship, its staff, and the way it is being run. If the ship inspector is not satisfied then he may call for a full survey by an independent surveyor.

The full survey by the independent surveyor appointed by the P&I Club would usually be working to a pro-forma set of guidelines provided by the club. The inspection would probably cover everything required for a classification and load-line survey and much more. The cargo-carrying compartments in particular are given very close attention.

If the surveyor was not satisfied with any aspect then the deficiencies would be notified to the Master/Chief Engineer, the P&I Club, and the shipowners. Those deficiencies, certainly if they impaired the seaworthiness of the ship, would have to be remedied prior to the vessel being accepted into the club. If the vessel was already entered in the club then the club cover could be suspended in part, or in full, until the defects were remedied.

If a vessel is found defective by one P&I Club then this should mean that no other club in the International Group would accept that ship until the defects are remedied. However, more co-operation is possibly required amongst the clubs to ensure that this

practice is strictly adhered to.

In this way the P&I Clubs are having a significant impact in encouraging shipowners to ensure that high standards of maintenance are set on board and that the ships are kept in good condition. This can be seen as positive loss prevention in a pro-active way by checking on the physical condition of the ships. In fact, some clubs are now starting to look closer at the people on board the ship when considering its general condition and assessing the risk.

What seems unfortunate, though, is that the club surveyor is duplicating what the classification society is, or should be, doing. Surely this cannot make sense in a market where money is short?

Some hull and machinery underwriters are also employing their own surveyors, often the Salvage Association, to also carry out condition surveys on their behalf—again duplicating what the club surveyor and classification society surveyor have done or are supposed to have done.

Charterers may also be involved in surveying the same parts of the same ship.

In fact the writer is aware of a recent case when the Master of a tanker was at his wit's end—his ship had undergone 19 surveys in a period of three months!

4.1.3. Port State control

In an attempt to set international minimum standards of conditions for ships, the United Nations were instrumental in setting up the system of port State control. Yet another survey!

Some ports strictly and vigorously enforce port State control regulations and requirements, others seem to turn a blind eye, or to concentrate on the easier targets— the northern European ships, for example, which they know will co-operate with them, ignoring the ships which are likely to cause problems.

Certainly this is a good initiative in principle and should be supported in an attempt to ensure that ships which are unseaworthy or inadequately maintained cannot trade.

Clearly, the question needs to be asked—why should port State control be necessary? Why is it that ships are found by port State control to be in seriously defective condition but, at the same time, fully classed and insured?

Is it beyond the bounds of possibility to have some sort of coordination?

4.1.4. Withdrawal of insurance cover

The ultimate weapon against a shipowner whose ship is in an unseaworthy and/or badly maintained state is to withdraw insurance cover. Clearly, any insurance cover, whether hull and machinery or P&I, becomes void if class is withdrawn or suspended.

A shipowner without insurance is unlikely to find any company prepared to charter his ship, or any cargo owner prepared to put his cargo on board, and it is very unlikely that any port would allow an uninsured ship to enter harbour.

On the face of it, therefore, the insurers themselves could have a significant effect in reducing claims by taking greater care over what they insure.

E

4.1.5. Self regulation

A very important question needs to be addressed by shipowners, ship managers and their insurers; are they prepared to regulate themselves and raise and maintain high standards of maintenance and operations? If not, national governments will legislate for them as happened in the USA with the OPA'90.

Certainly, a move in the right direction has been made by the ship management member companies, for example, of the International Ship Managers' Association (ISMA) by setting quality assurance standards. A number of national shipowners associations are trying hard to encourage the raising of standards, but there are others who are less than enthusiastic.

There is one thing for certain; life for the shipowner/ship manager will not be any easier if they force Brussels or some national government to start legislating on various matters which will affect the commercial operation of the ships. It must surely make sense for flag States and individual shipowners, ship managers and their associations to commit themselves to raising their standards so that there would be no necessity for national governments to impose their own legislation.

4.2.0. Human element in claims

The human element in claims has already been discussed in Section 3.5. above. In this section it is hoped that some suggestions can be put forward to help overcome the human element in claims.

4.2.1.0. Education and training

Before any progress can be made with education and training programmes it is imperative to have a labour force who will be receptive to the provision of such education and training courses. There is another saying: 'You can take a horse to the water but you cannot make him drink'!

In this section an attempt will be made to suggest how relevant education and training could be developed and implemented.

4.2.1.1. Current state of related education

It would appear that commercial, legal and business subjects are taught to senior marine students in nautical colleges around the world as part of the syllabus leading to their professional qualifications. However, in most cases it would seem that the subjects are taught at the most basic academic level by staff who have rarely had any practical experience working in the commerical, legal or insurance side of shipping.

Students learn the functions of bills of lading, but not what to do if a dispute arises between the way in which a shipper has described the goods and the Master's own observation of the condition of the cargo. The differences between voyage and time charter parties is explained but not, for example, what the Master's responsibilities are towards cargo under a New York Produce Exchange form charter party.

It is not being suggested that Masters and ship's officers should be trained to become lawyers or P&I claims handlers. What is being suggested for the

avoidance of many of these claims is for the Master and his officers to be provided with the necessary tools, by way of relevant education and training, for dealing with commercial or legal problems which may arise until outside help can be obtained or to be in a position to take such steps as would prevent the incident occurring in the first place.

To achieve this, it is suggested, it will be necessary to teach the teachers! Before that takes place there need to be changes to the relevant syllabus.

4.2.1.2. STCW Convention

The relevant syllabus of many maritime nations is based upon the STCW Convention as promulgated by the International Maritime Organization (the IMO). By its constitution, the IMO is primarily concerned with maritime safety aspects and marine environmental issues.

These topics are of paramount importance and it would certainly never be the wish, or intention, to reduce the emphasis given to these subjects. However, we should never lose sight of the fact that a merchant ship's very existence is as part of a commercial venture. It is suggested that the education and training of the Master and officers should not only include the important safety subjects but that these should be complemented by commercial subjects.

What does not seem to be recognised by some, is that there is no conflict at all between these important safety aspects and the commercial aspects of a well-run ship—they must complement each other.

If a shipowner attempts to save money, for so called 'commercial' reasons by sacrificing safety standards, whether it be by employing cheaper, poorly qualified, inexperienced crew or by cutting back on important maintenance or by allowing unsafe working practices, or whatever, then any savings made will be very much in the short term. That sort of 'commerical' approach will, as a natural consequence, lead to significant claims which in turn will lead to large increases in insurance premium— as already discussed in Section 2 of this document. It will also lead to a bad reputation in the market place, so that the good quality charterer would not wish to do business with such a shipowner, the shipper will not be at all happy to allow his cargo to be carried on board such a ship. As quality assurance becomes more and more significant in shipping, then those short-term 'commercial' operators will find it increasingly difficult to operate in a true commercial world where safety and high standards co-exist in harmony with the other aspects of the commercial venture.

Since, at present, the only attempt which has been made, on an international level, to introduce a syllabus covering basic minimum standards is the STCW Convention, then it is suggested that this syllabus should be expanded to cover the commercial, legal and insurance subjects.

At this time the STCW Convention is coming up for a full review and the writer suggests that the opportunity should not be lost for the shipping community, as well as other commercial and insurance interests, to encourage the IMO to incorporate such subjects into the new STCW Convention.

4.2.1.3. Liaison between nautical training establishments and the insurance industry

The P&I Clubs and the hull and machinery insurers handle vast quantities of claims and disputes on very diverse incidents. A tremendous wealth of experience, and expertise, is accumulated by the management and staff of the Clubs and underwriters; not only in how to deal with and settle such claims, but also how and why thse claims and disputes arose. They should, therefore be ideally placed to advise how such claims and incidents could be avoided or at least to advise how the consequences could be minimised if they did occur.

Up to now this wealth of experience has barely been tapped. A detailed discussion of the possibilities and potential of the issue can be found in the writer's report *The Human Element in Claims—What Role for the P&I Clubs?*.

From the research carried out for that report it became patently obvious that the vast majority of nautical training establishments—96% of those surveyed—confirmed that they would welcome, and that their students would benefit from, contact with the insurance industry.

The P&I correspondents, who are located in all major, and many minor ports, around the world, were also surveyed and 93% of those who participated in the survey confirmed that they would be prepared to establish contact with their local nautical training establishment or that they have a contact already.

There would appear to be a very real, prospect of the hands-on practical experience and expertise of the people dealing with many of the marine claims and disputes, helping in a positive and direct way in the education and training of seafarers in relevant loss prevention issues. This could complement the academic teaching of the college lecturers.

4.2.1.4. Co-operation within the shipping industry

It became apparent from the research carried out for *The Human Element in Claims— What Role for the P&I Clubs?* report that a considerable number of initiatives are being taken by many sectors and organisations within the shipping industry to try and deal with the problem of accidents and claims.

From the results of that survey, it became clear that all the relevant sectors of the maritime industry which participated confirmed a similar view that the vast majority of all accidents, claims and incidents arose as a result of human error, or at least had a human involvement.

Many different initiatives appear to be currently underway, both in isolation and as joint ventures attempting to deal with the human element in claims. This includes various forms of education and training programmes and also extends in one case, at least, to looking at the psychological and motivational aspects of multi-cultural crews.

Almost all sectors of the maritime industry surveyed seemed to be enthusiastically supportive of the idea of more co-operation between different sectors of the industry to try and deal with the problem of the human element in claims; indeed some very interesting proposals were put forward in order to progress the idea. This included a suggestions that industry could become more involved in nautical education.

4.2.1.5. Training courses

It may be that the incorporation of these commercial subjects, to a meaningful level, into the STCW Convention or other syllabus set by national government bodies cannot be accommodated or will be a long time coming. The reality is that the problem of rising claims and their consequences is facing the shipowner now—today! Relevant training courses, specifically designed for the internationally serving seafarer, are almost non-existent. Not quite though . . .

For the past four years, The North of England P&I Association, in conjunction with the South Tyneside Marine College, have run a unique and very successful distance learning course in P&I insurance which was written primarily for ships' Masters and senior officers. Whilst the course provides a first class introduction to P&I insurance, at the core of the course are practical loss prevention issues, including bills of lading and charter party problems and cargo claims.

Another important contribution is a series of annual seminars organised by the North East branch of The Nautical Institute in Newcastle on the general theme of 'The Mariner and the Maritime Law'. These seminars have become very popular and not only provide the mariner with the opportunity of attending a first class seminar, but also provide an opportunity for him to meet P&I claims adjusters, maritime lawyers, consultants, arbitrators, etc.

There is no reason at all why such seminars could not be organised and held anywhere in the world. The North East branch of the Nautical Institute will be pleased to assist with advice, based on their own experience, on how such seminars could be organised and structured.

Nautical training colleges around the world, possibly with the assistance of local P&I correspondents, could consider the possibility of running extra curricular courses.

4.2.1.6. Publications

Most P&I Clubs produce a variety of literature which they distribute to their own shipowner members and a restricted mailing list. Some of this literature is of a very high standard—e.g. the UK Club publication *Carefully to Carry*, which deals in depth with a number of commodities, their properties and characteristics, and provides guidance on carrying specific cargoes safely.

There is a wealth of literature which is likely to be produced from club and group circulars to newsletters, seminar papers, rule books etc. One question which should be asked is whether most of this literature ever arrives where it is intended; on board the ship?

Strenuous efforts should be made to ensure that the relevant publications do arrive on board ship. Care should be taken when preparing these publications to ensure that they are relevant to the seafarer and to ensure that what is being said is clear and will be easily understood. The use of case studies or examples are most useful methods of getting a particular point across.

4.2.2. Choice of Master, officers and crew

This is possibly the single most important issue when considering what can be done to prevent claims arising. Unfortunately it seems that all too often little regard is given to the choice of Master, officers and crew. A shipowner or ship manager sends details of their requirements to a manning agent and, usually, the required number of people are sent to the ship.

Frequently these crews place their loyalties with the manning agent rather than with the shipowner or ship manager.

If anything meaningful is to be done with the problem of claims then the first hurdle to overcome is to find a first class team of Master, officers and crew. The second hurdle is to keep that team!

The writer believes that an investment in people is the best investment that can possibly be made in the battle to solve the problem of claims. Once the right people are found and a climate is created whereby those people have an interest and an incentive to make a long term commitment to a particular ship or shipping company, then they will be receptive to appropriate education and training in loss prevention so that claims avoidance will come as a matter of course.

4.2.3. Size of the crew

It is certainly a truism that quality is much more important than quantity. However, even the most highly qualified, experienced, and motivated officers and crew will have limits to what is humanly possible and if there are simply not enough people to carry out the duties effectively then mistakes will be made, accidents will happen and claims will arise.

Accordingly, considerable care should be exercised when determining what may realistically be considered minimum crew numbers on board.

4.2.4. Terms of employment

It is suggested that the best way to achieve staff loyalty, motivate personnel and achieve a harmonious working relationship is to offer reasonable and attractive terms of employment. Certainly financial remuneration is part of the equation but of equal or greater importance is 'job security' and continuity of employment. By providing company contracts of employment a 'we' feeling can be created—that sense of belonging—with which will come commitment to the job and the company.

4.2.5. Inter-cultural communications

There are good and bad crews of every nationality but, regardless of an individual's ability, there are very few good crews where many different nationalities and cultures are mixed with little regard to interaction.

If accidents and claims are to be minimised, then there needs to be on board a harmonious working relationship between Master, officers and crew.

Accordingly, considerable thought must be given to the possible consequences of mixing nationalities and cultures on board.

It is not unusual for two different nationalities, with a mutual respect for each other, to work well together. The problems arise when that status quo is broken and a third or fourth nationality/culture is introduced which leads to friction and animosity.

4.2.6. Quality management systems (on board ship and ashore)

Any quality system is only as good as the people implementing it. Few would question the advantages of a good quality management system to bring about a more efficient, cost effective approach to the job, which, if properly implemented, should help to reduce accidents and claims. However, a poorly constructed system or a system which is being imposed upon an unwilling, uninterested workforce is perceived as the source of even more work to do, more forms to fill in and more time consuming procedures to follow. Such a system is unlikely to succeed. Again, to a lesser extent, much depends on the attitude of the Master, officers and crew to the ship, the shipping company and the answer to that most basic of questions: 'What is in it for me ?'.

With a permanent labour force then the possibility exists for close involvement by the sea staff in the drafting and implementation of the QA system. This is a 'must' if the system is to work on board.

4.2.7. Motivation

Much has already been said, in section 3.5.4. and elsewhere, about motivational issues.

The bottom line is that if many of the accidents and claims are to be avoided or prevented in future then there must be sufficient motivation amongst a shipowner's staff both ashore and afloat.

If some of the suggestions put forward in the early parts of this section were implemented then motivation would be a natural by-product and the natural consequence would be that accidents and claims would decrease.

4.3.0.Exercising due diligence to make the vessel seaworthy

The obligation upon the carrier to 'exercise due diligence' to make the ship seaworthy is set out in Article III Rule 1 of the Hague/Hague Visby Rules:

Article III

1. The carrier shall be bound before and at the beginning of the voyage to exercise due diligence to:-

(a) Make the ship seaworthy.
(b) Properly man, equip and supply the ship.
(c) Make the holds, refrigerating and cool chambers, and all other parts of the ship in which goods are carried, for their reception, carriage and preservation.

A seaworthy ship could, perhaps be defined as follows:

'A ship is seaworthy if it can embark on the voyage and

proceed to sea in a condition fit to encounter the normal conditions of the marine environment without the risk of danger or damage to the ship or cargo arising out of the failure of the ship itself or from the normal environmental conditions.'

This simply means the ship must be in a fit condition with regards to its:

- Hull and machinery.
- Cargo holds and cargo equipment.
- Manning and procedures.

Importance of due diligence

By exercising due diligence the shipowner will be expected to take good care to make the ship seaworthy before each voyage.

If cargo loss or damage occurs during the voyage the shippers, or rightful owners of the cargo will pose the question as to whether this was the result of not taking good care to make the vessel seaworthy.

If it can be shown that:

(i) any deficiency should have been detected by careful checking of the vessel before the voyage commenced, and
(ii) a careful owner would have remedied or repaired that deficiency before allowing the vessel to proceed to sea

then the shipowner will be liable for the loss and damage.

Once the cargo interests have established proper grounds for a claim and substantiated an allegation of unseaworthiness, it is then up to the carrier to demonstrate that due diligence was exercised to make the vessel seaworthy.

The Master, as the legal representatives of the shipowner on board the vessel, is responsible for ensuring that due diligence is exercised and all the necessary checks or repairs were carried out. Some companies may, however, have superintendents who supervise this work and approve any repair or maintenance work that needs to be carried out.

4.3.1.Maintenance systems

A ship is a very complex structure, containing a vast number of items of machinery, equipment, and fittings that all require inspection and maintenance to ensure they will function satisfactorily.

Classification societies and State legislation require a vessel to undergo a number of detailed periodic surveys carried out by approved surveyors to ensure the vessel remains in a satisfactory condition with respect to her hull, machinery, equipment, lifesaving and fire-fighting appliances, and radio equipment. Even if a ship possesses valid certificates issued by these surveyors, it is still necessary for the carrier to show that checks to ensure that the ship was, in fact, seaworthy and, particularly, cargo worthy were carried out.

The level of checking that should take place before each voyage does not go to the lengths of a major survey, but it does require that the Master and crew have carried out the checks in a professional and seaman-like manner.

Routine maintenance around the ship should in any case, be carried out methodically and on a continuous basis, although, for practical reasons, some of this work can only be carried out in port. Operational experience may well point to items of equipment needing checking at relatively short intervals.

The whole aim of carrying out checks is to identify where maintenance and repairs are needed in order to ensure all equipment will function properly until it can next be safely inspected and serviced. Any repairs carried out should also be thoroughly checked to ensure they have been carried out properly.

If a piece of equipment fails, the assumption will be that it was not checked properly. The shipowner will need to show the failure of the equipment was not due to lack of checking and would not have been discovered by a reasonable inspection.

From what has been said above it will be seen why it is important to carry out checks of the ship, machinery, equipment, cargo holds and cargo equipment before embarking on a passage.

The responsibility for this lies with the shipowner and will only be effective if there is good shipboard organisation with appropriate guidance from the shipowner or his management team.

Clearly it has to be recognised that the Master maintains a very important role in the shipboard organisation. No organisation will be effective however, unless there are suitably trained and qualified persons on board.

The Master's main role in exercising due diligence will be to:

- Delegate, to responsible officers, the checking of all fittings, items of machinery and equipment on deck, in the engine room and in the cargo holds. Despite delegating these tasks, the Master remains, at all times, responsible, and the work is carried out under his supervision.

- Ensure that procedures are adopted that will enable checking and maintenance to be carried out efficiently as regularly as is required.

- Ensure that suitable records are kept of all checks, maintenance and repair work carried out.

- Discuss with all his officers the reasons why it is important to carry out proper checks.

The whole purpose of these checks is to ensure that, before the commencement of each voyage, the vessel and cargo are in all respects in a seaworthy condition.

4.3.2.Patent steel hatch covers

(Special acknowledgement is given to Captain John R Knott for much of the material of this section)

There was a time when the phrase 'weather-deck steel hatch covers' referred to one general design and one manufacturer or licensee using that manufacturer's name.

Nowadays, weather-deck steel hatch covers come in a wide range of designs and types, sub-types and adaptations. The most common form of steel cover is the type with single-pull, rolling panels, all panels stowing at the after end or forward end of the hatchway when open.

Weather-deck steel hatch covers rely for their watertightness upon the perimeter compression bar surrounding the hatch coaming mating with some form of softer surface in the perimeter of the covers, and upon the transverse mating surfaces between the hatch cover cross-joints being provided with an equally effective compression seal system. Lack of attention to these two aspects probably gives rise to more claims for sea water damage to cargo than any other.

At the perimeter, that is at the port and starboard sides and forward and aft end coamings, water-tightness is achieved by rubber packing—held in a retaining channel—acting vertically downward onto a steel compression bar.

In all double drainage systems, it is most important to keep the drain holes and tubes free of obstruction; for blockage will cause water to back up in the secondary drainage channels and then flow over the upward extension of the hatch coaming plate into the cargo compartment. If that upward extension is, in any event, structurally damaged, draining water will undoubtedly run down the coaming plate and damage cargo below.

There are many different methods of making the transverse cross-joints watertight by means of a single-drainage system. If water gets past the compression bar due to the vessel working heavily in the seaway, it has nowhere but downward to drain and will drip into the cargo spaces below when heavy flexing of the covers may cause loss of compression bar contact. Nevertheless, these methods are still most common and must be maintained with care.

There are also different methods of double-drainage cross-joints. The difference here lies in the principle of primary and secondary drainage. If water gets past the compression bar seal, it drips into the secondary drainage channel from which it drains to the coaming secondary channel and, from there, via the drain valves to the deck. Again, it is most important to keep drain holes clean and clear of obstruction.

Some systems are noticeably more efficient than others, but there are four aspects of most designs which require constant care, inspection and regular maintenance if watertight integrity is to be maintained:

1. Packing material
2. Retaining channels
3. Compression bars and inner coaming bars
4. Cross-joint wedges.

If there are any golden rules concerning weather-deck steel hatchcovers, they can probably be encapsulated as follows:

(a) Keep all mating surfaces clean, inspect them regularly and replace packing material wherever and whenever necessary, with particular attention to the degree of permanent set and material degradation.

(b) Keep all drain-holes, drain-pipes and drain-valves clear and free of scale and cargo residues.

(c) Do not allow scale to develop behind and around the packing material. Maintain all compression surfaces and bars free of physical distortion, damage and scale.

(d) Follow the manufacturer's instructions for operation and maintenance, apply cross-joint wedges at their designed-for compression; wherever possible use the guaranteed spare parts and the technical expertise available from the manufacturers themselves.

(e) The successful testing of steel hatch covers in service, by the accepted use of hose, chalk and ultrasound should not discourage the ship's officers concerned from maintaining continued vigilance in respect of the foregoing or, indeed, in general.

This is not a counsel of perfection, unobtainable in practice. Rather, it is the reasonable, practical programme necessary to keep weather-deck steel hatch covers in sound, sea-going condition and, if proper records of maintenance are kept, of undoubted assistance in establishing due diligence on behalf of shipowners and shipboard personnel.

4.3.3. Preloading inspection of the cargo-carrying compartments

Under the Hague Rules, the carrier is obliged to exercise due diligence to make the ship seaworthy before it puts to sea. Exercising due diligence means taking good care.

If problems arise on board during the course of a voyage, the test for determining whether or not the carrier has taken good care to make the ship seaworthy is as follows:

1. Should the defect have come to light by the careful checking of the ship before the voyage began?

2. If so, would a careful owner have remedied that defect before sending the ship, with her cargo on board, to sea?

In order to ensure that good care has been taken, there is no substitute for the proper and regular checking of all aspects of the ship and its manning, of all work, maintenance and repairs carried out on board. Moreover, all procedures and standing instructions which are in force on board should be reviewed in order to ensure that these are adequate and well suited for the ship putting to sea and safely carrying its cargo. All checks and regular maintenance work should be carried out as regularly as necessary to avoid failure in the vessel, its personnel and its procedures.

The master and the crew should not rely on the findings of the outside examiners such as classification society or underwriters' surveyors. These surveyors have different interests and do not usually work to the same guidelines, standards or requirements.

In general, particular attention should be paid to inspecting items such as: hatch covers, cargo doors, access ramps, cargo holds, cargo tanks, sounding pipes, air pipes, bilges, scuppers, valves, cargo pumps, heating coils, inert gas system, refrigeration plant, derricks, cranes, standing and running rigging with fixtures, lashing points and all other loading and discharging gear.

4.3.4.Record keeping

All of the checks and regular maintenance work carried out by the crew should be properly recorded and documented. If something does go wrong and cargo is lost or damaged, then the presumption will be that the carrier has not taken good care to make the vessel seaworthy. In order to refute this presumption, the carrier must have evidence in the form of log books, work schedules, work books, work specifications, accounts, standing instructions, reports and contemporaneous correspondence to show that good care has been taken to make the vessel seaworthy.

4.4.0. Carrier's obligation to take care of the cargo

As was mentioned earlier, an obligation imposed by the Hague and Hague Visby Rules is that the carrier shall:-

'. . . .(subject to the provisions of Article IV) . . . properly and carefully load, handle, stow, keep, care for, and discharge the goods carried . . . ' (Article III Rule 2).

This obligation continues throughout the period within which the carrier is responsible. The period of responsibility is generally extended under the Hamburg Rules.

The exact stage at which the carrier becomes responsible and ceases to be responsible may not always be readily apparent. This can only be determined by provisions contained in bill of lading, the charter party (if appropriate), or by local custom and law.

A cargo may have been handled by several parties during its carriage. If loss or damage arises, it will be necessary to establish who was responsible for the care of the cargo at the time the loss or damage occurred.

Very often the carrier will be responsible for all the stages of cargo handling operations i.e. the loading, stowage, carriage and discharge. If all of these are done carefully and properly, then it should avoid the cargo being damaged or lost in transit.

In addition to the obligation to take good care to make the ship seaworthy, the Hague Visby Rules also impose an obligation on the carrier to take good care to look after the cargo from the time it is entrusted to him until the time that it is delivered to the receiver (see Article III Rule 2). If the cargo, at the time of delivery, is lost or damaged, the carrier will be called upon to explain how the loss or damage occurred.

The period of time during which the carrier must take good care of the cargo can only be determined by looking at many different factors. The relevant contracts (for example, the charter-party and the bill of lading) will usually determine the period of time during which the carrier remains responsible for the cargo. However, local laws may override or refuse to recognise contractual provisions which conflict with local regulations or practice.

The obligation on the carrier is to do everything necessary to deliver the cargo to the receiver in the same good order and condition as when it was entrusted to him. The carrier, therefore, must ensure that all cargo handling operations including the loading, stowing, carrying and discharging are done properly and carefully. Moreover, the carrier must ensure that the cargo is properly cared for and kept so that the condition of the cargo is maintained. The Master should be fully aware of any special attention that the cargo may require. Information and instructions with regard to the treatment of cargo should be sought in writing from the shipper. If the Master has any reservations about this information, he should request the assistance of owners or their local agents who may appoint an independent surveyor, or expert.

The carrier may be held responsible for any problems which arise out of any of the cargo handling operations which he has contracted to undertake or arrange. In addition, the carrier will be held responsible for any cargo handling operations for which, under the local laws, he is primarily responsible, whether or not he has contractually undertaken to do these operations. Therefore, it is essential that the Master is aware of the local laws, customs and practices as well as the provisions in the relevant contracts which relate to cargo handling operations. The owners' local agents or local P&I Correspondents should be able to advise him of local laws which dictate that particular cargo operations fall within the carrier's responsibility.

If a particular cargo handling operation, which is the carrier's responsibility, is not carried out properly, the carrier will be unable to avoid liabilities if loss or damage occurs to the cargo even if the Master inserts into a statement of facts an endorsement stating that the carrier is not responsible. Such endorsements may be of evidential value for indemnity proceedings and the Master may note on the statement of facts or in correspondence any irregularities relating to the cargo handling operations.

The standard of care required of the carrier is independent of the usual custom or practice. The carrier's obligation is to look after the cargo properly and carefully and it will be no defence to a claim for damage to say that the cargo was carried in accordance with usual practice.

In order to avoid liability, if cargo is lost or damaged, the carrier will have to demonstrate that his obligation of caring for the cargo has been fully and properly discharged. Therefore, the Master must ensure that all cargo handling operations are accurately recorded and fully documented so that the carrier will be able to bring forward the evidence necessary to defend the claim.

4.4.1.Familiarisation with the intended cargo

Publications are usually, or should be, carried on board which will provide information about the properties and stowage requirements of particular cargoes. However, they cannot always be relied upon to be up-to-date or exhaustive. For example, new products and commodities are increasingly being shipped. Also, changes in methods of stowage and care of a cargo may be appropriate in the light of operating experiences within the industry.

Shippers frequently give the Master carrying instructions which should be complied with unless they are clearly in error.

If doubt exists about the proper carriage of the cargo, the Master should immediately discuss the matter with the shipowner, shipper or charterer or, if necessary, seek advice from an independent expert of from the Club.

4.4.2.Planning the loading

In section 4.3 above emphasis was laid on the importance of making the vessel cargo worthy and ensuring the holds are fit to receive cargo. As a matter of routine, holds should be inspected by the ship's officers and an entry made in the log book. As there are many cargoes that may, during carriage, become damaged by being loaded into improperly prepared hatches, etc., the Master should consider obtaining a surveyor's hold condition report prior to loading certain cargoes.

Some vessels carry cargoes that require machinery and special equipment to be working correctly and efficiently before loading can start—refrigerated cargoes, for example. For these types of vessel a survey should be carried out by a classification surveyor or other competent person who will issue a certificate stating that the machinery or equipment and holds are in a fit condition and suitable for the carriage of the cargo.

To ensure that the cargo is loaded in an efficient and satisfactory manner the cargo plan and loading instructions should take into account the following criteria:

● The holds are properly prepared for the cargo.

● Loading and discharge rotations are taken into account.

● Special stowage requirements are followed.

● Cross-contamination of cargo is avoided.

● There is adequate stability at all stages of loading.

● The correct cargo is being loaded as per booking list.

● The cargo is tallied on board.

● Loading is stopped and the hatches covered during periods of rain or other adverse weather conditions.

4.3.Inspecting the cargo prior to and during loading

One of the main functions of a bill of lading, in addition to it being a receipt for the goods, is that it contains evidence of the apparent order and condition (and the quantity or weight) of the goods loaded on board the vessel. Article III Rule 3 of the Hague/Hague—Visby Rules sets out this obligation which, at the relevant part, reads:

'. . . After receiving the goods into his charge the carrier or the master or agent of the carrier shall, on demand of the shipper, issue to the shipper a bill of lading showing among other things:

. . . (c) The apparent order and condition of the goods . . . '.

It is of paramount importance therefore that the Master or the delegated officer responsible should carefully carry out a reasonable inspection of the cargo prior to and during loading.

The Master is not expected to be an expert with regard to the quality of any particular commodity but he is expected to be capable of carrying out a 'reasonable' inspection and noting any 'obvious' defects. It is not always easy to define what is 'reasonable' or 'obvious'. The question which a Master should ask himself is 'can this particular piece or parcel of cargo be accurately described as in "apparent good order and condition" '? If the answer is No, then a suitable descriptive remark should be considered which will accurately describe the 'apparent order and condition'. If in doubt the services of an experienced surveyor should be considered at an early stage.

There are at least two very good reasons why a Master should exercise considerable care over this matter.

The first relates to a further function of the bill of lading i.e. that it is a document of title to the goods. This means that the shipper, by endorsing the bill of lading, can transfer the property and ownership of the goods to a third party.

In this regard the third party buyer will rely upon any statements made in the bill of lading including statements about the apparent order and condition of the cargo. Consequently if the bill of lading stated that the cargo was in 'apparent good order and condition' and the cargo outturned in anything less than 'apparent good order and condition' then the receiver would probably have a very good claim against the carrier. Indeed Article III Rule 4 of the Hague Visby Rules makes the point quite clear:

'. . . Such a bill of lading shall be prima facie evidence of the receipt by the carrier of the goods as therein described in accordance with paragraph 3(a), (b) and (c). However, proof to the contrary shall not be admissible when the bill of lading has been transferred to a third party acting in good faith . . . '.

With an endorsed or transferred bill of lading, a third party has bought the goods on the strength of the details shown on the bill and, accordingly it becomes conclusive evidence of the apparent condition of the goods at the time of shipment. The shipowner cannot, in this case, avoid the claim by showing that the details in the bill of lading were incorrect.

The second reason why the Master should exercise considerable care over this obligation is that if cargo is loaded and it is known, or should be known, that it is in a defective condition and clean bills of lading are issued then the shipowners insurance with his P&I Club could be prejudiced. Each Club has its own rule covering this particular matter and North of England P&I Club Rule 19(17)(D) reads, at the relevant part, as follows:

'. . . Unless the Directors in the exercise of their

discretion shall otherwise determine no claim on the Association shall be allowed in respect of a member's liability arising out of:

. . . (vi) A bill of lading, way bill or other document containing or evidencing the contract of carriage issued with the knowledge of the Member or the Master with an incorrect description of the cargo or its quantity or its condition . . . '.

It is very important therefore to ensure that damaged cargo is either rejected before it comes on board, or a careful note made of the damaged goods, including all identification marks on the mate's receipts—see figure 22 (page 64).

A point not always fully appreciated is that any damage done by the stevedores, once the cargo has passed into the custody of the carrier, will probably be the responsibility of the carrier. As a consequence cargo interests may validly pursue a claim against the carrier. It is important for ship's officers to keep a close watch on stevedores to ensure cargo is loaded carefully. If damage to cargo does occur, the Master should write to the stevedores, with full details, holding them responsible and send a copy to the shipowner and, if appropriate, the charterers.

For tankers it is important that:

● Cargo samples are drawn at regular intervals, preferably at the manifold. Samples should be labelled and clearly show where and also the time when they were drawn.

● After completion of loading, careful ullage and temperature measurements should be taken to enable a calculation of the cargo received on board to be made.

4.4.4.Exceptions clauses and mate's receipts

As was mentioned previously, the Master and his officers are not expected to be experts on every type of cargo that may be loaded.

It is expected, however, that they will be competent and be able to identify something obviously wrong with the cargo after a reasonable inspection.

Following from this reasonable inspection the Master, or duly delegated officer, should prepare an exceptions list or appropriate mate's receipt.

The kind of things which should be looked for would include, for example:

● Wet bales or bags.

● Stained or contaminated goods.

● Frozen cargo which has partially thawed.

● Discoloured or mouldy grain.

● Foreign material in a bulk cargo.

● Broken or damaged goods.

● Rust on shipments of steel.

This last example (shipment of steel) has resulted in so many claims due to rust damage that most P&I Clubs pay for loading surveys on these cargoes. The surveyor assists the ship's officers to identify damage

and rusting before and during loading and in drafting a suitable exceptions list. This is then used to assist with the clausing of the mate's receipts and/or the bills of lading.

An important document used in preparing bills of lading is the mate's receipts which is a receipt, given and signed by the mate, for goods actually received on board the ship. The mate's receipts must be carefully prepared and give a description of the cargo, including the quantity (number of items and/or the weight), distinguishing marks, grade and any other relevant information.

The bill of lading will be prepared from details shown on the mate's receipt and it is important that the particulars shown on the receipt truthfully and accurately describe the apparent order and condition of the goods at the time of loading. Shipowner's agents, for example may be given written authorisation by the Master to sign bills of lading on behalf of the shipowner in accordance with the details on the mate's receipts.

An example of such a letter is provided at Appendix II.

Where justified and appropriate the mate should clause the mate's receipt i.e. add appropriate qualifying remarks about the cargo.

For example, if some cargo loaded is damaged the mate's receipt should be claused with the number and identifying marks of all the damaged goods and the nature of the damage.

Depending upon circumstances, if the condition of the cargo is found to be unsatisfactory it should be:

● Rejected and not loaded.

or

● Loaded, but full details noted on the mate's receipts and bills of lading. If the agents are to issue and sign such bills they should be provided with clear and unambiguous instructions.

4.4.5.Rejecting damaged cargo

Perhaps the greatest vigilance required by the ship's officer is checking the condition of the cargo. This is particularly important when 'clean bills of lading' have to be signed. This simply means that all the cargo loaded must be in prime condition and not damaged or contaminated in any way. In these circumstances the ship's officers will have to reject, and prevent from being loaded, cargo which is not in first-class condition, otherwise tremendous problems will arise when it comes to signing bills of lading and the shipowner could be exposed to claims for substantial damages.

It is vitally important that the Master is advised prior to commencement of loading that clean bills of lading are required.

4.4.6.Compatibility of cargoes

As a general rule; the carrier becomes responsible for the safe custody of the cargo once it is handed over to him. This may take place ashore but, more frequently, it is assumed to take place when the cargo passes over the ship's rail during the loading operation.

If the cargo becomes damaged after it passes into the custody of the carrier then, quite reasonably, the carrier is going to be liable to the owner of the cargo for the consequences unless he has a very good excuse.

There are a number of ways in which the cargo might become damaged but one frequently recurring type of claim arises as a result of one cargo being contaminated by another.

Two of the most serious problems of this type are tainting and wet/moisture damage.

Tea, pepper, dairy produce and other such commodities are readily tainted by other cargoes in the same compartment and will also lose their commercial value.

If care has not been exercised in segregating incompatible cargoes and taint damage occurs then it will be very difficult indeed for a carrier successfully to repudiate liability for a claim which would surely come forward. There would clearly have been a basic failure to care for the cargo.

In a similar way if, for example, kiln dried timber, which has a very low moisture content was stowed in the same compartment as wet or un-dried timber, it will readily take up moisture given off by the wet timber and as such, become damaged and lose its commercial value.

This problem is frequently encountered when loading steel. Some steel arrives at the ship straight from the factory or from undercover storage.

The next parcel to arrive may have been standing out in the rain or maybe covered with snow or may arrive in an uncovered railway truck for example— and the parcel is 'wet before shipment'.

Clearly the bill of lading should carry a remark to include the pre-shipment wetted condition but if that wet cargo is then loaded into the same compartment as the dry cargo very serious problems will inevitably arise. The wet steel will, either directly or indirectly, cause the dry, sound, steel to become contaminated with moisture which will, in a short space of time, cause rusting. Again if that happens then the carrier is unlikely to have any available case in his defence to claims brought by the owners of the dry steel—the carrier had failed to properly care for that cargo whilst it was on his custody.

It is important for the Master to:

● Identify those cargoes which are likely to be damaged by cross contamination.

● Arrange to load cargoes which can result in cross contamination different compartments or hatches.

● Seek advice immediately if in doubt about the properties of a cargo.

4.4.7. Measuring the quantity of cargo

In the case of some cargoes, checking the quantity loaded is relatively easy; bagged cargoes, for example, can be counted (tallied) as they come aboard.

(A suggested schedule for checking the integrity of a physical tally of bagged cargoes can be found at Appendix I) other cargoes, particularly bulk dry or liquid cargoes, cannot be tallied and quantity figures are usually those supplied by the shippers, based on using a variety of measuring devices such as weigh bridges, silo bins, railway truck and barge volumes, conveyor belt scales, flow meters, sounding of shore tanks.

In these circumstances the question is, should the Master sign the bill of lading accepting the shipper's figures?

The Hague and Hague Visby Rules assume the carrier will check the details put into the Bill of Lading. Signing the bills of lading without taking steps to check the quantity will expose the carrier to shortage claims by third parties.

The relevant part of Article III Rule 3 of the Hague— Hague Visby Rules read as follows:

' . . . .after receiving the goods into his charge the carrier or the Master or agent of the carrier shall, on demand of the shipper, issue to the shipper a bill of lading showing among other things:

(b) Either the number of packages or pieces, or the quantity, or weight, as the case may be, as furnished in writing by the shipper . . . .

. . . .Provided that no carrier, Master or agent of the carrier shall be bound to state or show in the bill of lading any marks, number, quantity, or weight which he has reasonable ground for suspecting not accurately to represent the goods actually received, or which he has had no reasonable means of checking . . . .'

Entering a remark on the bills of lading with statements such as:

'quantity unknown' or 'shipper's figures said to weigh . . . ' may however, greatly assist shipowners in defending shortage claims, but may not always provide a total defence.

A ship can take some practical steps to check bulk cargo quantities loaded for example:

● Conducting a detailed draught survey and displacement calculation at the loading port is the only effective means of checking the shipper's figures for dry bulk carriers.

● The normal procedure for liquid bulk cargoes is to conduct an accurate ullage inspection on completion of loading.

It is not easy to give definitive advice on the exact degree of accuracy that should be accepted, for much will depend upon the trade in which the vessel is engaged, the size of vessel, the type of cargo, the condition of the sea state when the draught survey was carried out and many other parameters.

Most arbitrators and judges would recognise that the methods available to the Master for checking the quantity of bulk cargo loaded are subject to certain tolerances which are likely to result in small discrepancies between the ship's figures and the shore figure and these may be taken into account if any alleged shortage claim is made.

As a general rule anything other than minute differences between the shippers and the draught survey figures should be investigated further; if the discrepancy is significant and cannot be accounted for, the Master should consider:

● Deleting the B/L figure and inserting the ship's figure.

- Endorsing the B/L with the remark: 'X tons in dispute'.
- Refuse to sign the B/L and pass it to the agents with appropriate instructions.
- Tearing it up and issuing his own B/L.

If the shipper or charterer makes it difficult or impossible for the Master to deal with the differences in the ways suggested above the Master should immediately contact his owner and/or refer to matter to the P&I Club or its local correspondent.

4.4.8. Signing bills of lading

Clearly the bill of lading is an extremely important document when it comes to dealing with claims relating to shortage or condition of cargo. In fact, many claims might be avoided altogether if greater care was taken in issuing bills of lading.

The bill of lading is usually a shipowners document and it is the Master or shipowner's agent who signs the bill of lading on behalf of the shipowner.

Article III Rule 4 of the Hague Rules assumes that the carrier can and will check the particulars which are to be put into a bill of lading.

There are a number of very important points which the Master should consider before signing a bill of lading:

- Quantity of cargo
- Description and condition of the cargo
- Date
- Description of voyage
- Terms and conditions
- Payment of freight

The first two points were dealt with, in some depth, in sections 4.4.3. and 4.4.7. above. The other points are important though and are worth considering.

Date

The bill of lading must be dated when the cargo was loaded. Third parties make commercial decisions based on the correctness of this date and, if a loss occurs as a result, the owners will be liable. This could prejudice a shipowner's insurance cover with his P&I Club. The relevant part of North of England P&I Club Rule 19 (17) (D) reads as follows:

'Unless the Directors in the exercise of their discretion shall otherwise determine no claim on the Association shall be allowed in respect of a Member's liability arising out of:
. . . . (v) The issue of an ante-dated or post-dated bill of lading, way bill or other document containing or evidencing the contract of carriage . . . .'

Description of voyage

The voyage or destination stated in the bill of lading must be consistent with any charter party governing the vessel's employment or with any voyage instructions. The ship must also be capable of safely reaching the port of destination.

Terms and conditions

The bill of lading may indicate the shipment of cargo is being carried under the terms of a charter-party, if so, it should clearly identify the relevant charter-party.

Payment of freight

If a bill of lading is marked 'freight paid' or 'freight prepaid' it could represent a receipt for both cargo and freight money. The Master must have good evidence that freight has been paid or be instructed by owners or time charterers before signing such a Bill.

Letters of indemnity and issuing clean bills of lading

One related issue which is also worth considering is the problem faced by the Master when asked to accept a letter of indemnity in exchange for a clean bill of lading when cargo has been shipped in anything other than apparent good order and condition.

The Master is usually asked to accept such a letter shortly before completing loading and sailing. The shippers or charterers can apply considerable pressure on a Master to accept such a letter, with threats or suggestions of delays, and of putting the vessel off hire.

In fact, letters of indemnity are not readily enforceable and are frequently considered by the courts as an attempt to perpetrate a fraud, and owners end up with a valueless piece of paper in return for issuing a very valuable bill of lading.

In section 4.4.3. above it was pointed out that the cover provided by the P&I Club for liabilities in respect of cargo could be seriously prejudiced if 'clean' bills of lading are issued against a letter of indemnity when the cargo is known to have been loaded in a defective condition.

When faced with this sort of problem the Master would be well advised to immediately contact his shipowner or the P&I Club's nearest correspondent for assistance.

4.4.9. Use of surveyors

Some Masters have little hesitation in calling in the assistance of a surveyor for the slightest of problems. Other Masters are very reluctant to call for a surveyor however serious the problem might be; they seem to adopt an attitude that they are conceding some sort of personal failure by having to call in help—it is a matter of pride! The proper time to call in the help of a surveyor probably lies somewhere between these two extremes.

The services of surveyors tend to be expensive and the first Master would probably come under criticism if he was continually calling in surveyors for jobs which he and his officers should have been capable of solving themselves. On the other hand, the Master who failed to call in the help of a surveyor or called him in when it was too late to remedy the problem, would come under even greater criticism.

Certainly if the Master is genuinely in doubt about a situation or a serious dispute is developing, then he should not hesitate to request the help of a surveyor, even if it is only to provide a second opinion to back up the position the master wishes to adopt.

Clearly, if time allows, the Master should consult with his shipowners and/or charterers and/or the local correspondent of the P&I Club.

4.4.10 Local P&I correspondent

To enable the P&I Club to be represented in all the major ports of the world, and in many lesser ports, and to provide a global service to its members, the Club uses correspondents or representatives, not agents, since this term has certain legal implications.

The correspondents may be local maritime lawyers, specialist P&I Club representatives, ship's agents with suitably qualified personnel or, in some cases, surveyors.

Correspondents provide a variety of services but, basically, they are appointed because of their local knowledge, in the widest possible sense of that term, and their ability to assist and co-ordinate the handling of a problem locally, in the front line, to protect the member's position.

The club correspondent should be called in whenever it is clear that an incident has occurred which is likely to result in a claim against the P&I Association, or when the member/Master is in doubt about a particular problem of a P&I nature, when time does not permit them to make direct contact with the Association. The correspondent will appoint surveyors, lawyers, consultants, specialists etc., as may be necessary usually, if time allows, after checking with the P&I Club.

4.4.11 Caring for the cargo during the voyage

After the cargo has been carefully loaded and stowed on board, it requires looking after so that it will be delivered in the same order and condition as it was when loaded.

Some cargoes require little attention during the voyage; iron ore for example. Other cargoes require a great deal of attention and lack of care and attention can lead to substantial cargo damage and claims.

The problems associated with condensation and ventilation will be dealt with seperately in the next section. However, there are, other, frequently recurring problems; one of which is the problem associated with overheating/cooling:

Many dry cargoes generate heat themselves, which can result in spontaneous combustion and fire damage to the cargo—certain types of coal and fertilizer for example. Refrigerated cargoes and some bulk liquid cargoes need to be carried within a specified temperature band. If the temperature is allowed to fall below or rise above the temperature parameters, the cargo quality may deteriorate and lose its commercial value. If this has occurred because of some failure on the part of those on board who are commissioned with caring for the cargo then it is unlikely that the shipowner will successfully defend a resultant claim.

To avoid cargo damage and claims it is important that the following precautions are taken and checks made:

● Properties of the cargo are fully known.

● Regular monitoring of cargo and hold temperature

is carried out. If dangerous temperature rises are detected, appropriate action can be taken.

● A detailed record is kept of hold or cargo temperatures and action taken.

● Expert advice is sought when appropriate.

4.4.12 Ventilation

Unless condensation problems are fully understood, considerable damage to cargo can take place. Not carrying out ventilation, or ventilating the holds at the wrong time are the main reason for condensation problems.

Cargo can get wet by water vapour condensing onto the cargo (cargo sweat) or by water vapour condensing onto the ship's steelwork and dripping onto the cargo (ship's sweat). To avoid cargo damage the ship must establish the type of sweating that is likely to occur and adjust the ventilation requirements accordingly. A popular misconception regarding ventilation which seems to exist in some quarters is: 'if the weather is fine—ventilate!'.

This is ill founded and can have disastrous results.

The factors which govern the type of sweating that will take place are:

● Air and dew point temperatures both within the hold and outside the hold.

● Sea temperature.

● Whether the ship has loaded in a cold climate and is making a passage to a warm climate or vice versa.

● Nature of the cargo.

Whether the ship uses natural, fan assisted natural or a hold air drying system of ventilation; a record of temperatures, dew points and the times that ventilation was carried out is a valuable way of showing that the cargo was being properly cared for. Indeed such records will be of vital importance if a sweat damage claim is to be successfully defended.

There are, of course occasions when ventilation has to be restricted due to the bad weather and it is during these periods that condensation damage can take place. During these periods, not only should temperatures continue to be taken, but also full particulars of the actual weather and sea state should be recorded in the log book. Photograph or video recordings can be extremely useful evidence if a Master wishes to demonstrate why ventilation was restricted.

The importance of such records for evidential purposes cannot be over emphasised.

4.4.13 At the discharge port

Problems frequently arise at the discharge port when cargo interests claim the weight of cargo discharged is difference from the weight loaded. Unless the ship can account for the difference, cargo interests will claim for loss or shortage of cargo.

Again, a well conducted outturn draught or ullage survey by the ship will be of great help, together with a signed statement by an independent witness confirming that there is no cargo remaining on board.

There may well be other reasons that could account for the difference. Some cargoes such as concentrates, ore and coal can contain considerable quantities of water when loaded. During the voyage, much of this water will settle out and find its way into the bilge. This water represents the lost cargo, so it is essential to keep accurate bilge sounding records and the times when bilges are pumped.

4.4.14. Letters of protest

Sometimes it is necessary for the Master to send a letter of protest or reservation to stevedores, shippers or charterers. A letter of protest is simply a declaration by the Master of a statement of facts and may, if appropriate, hold another party responsible for some loss or damage that has already occurred, or is likely to occur to the ship or cargo.

By itself, noting heavy weather protest will not provide a defence, as evidence is still required. It is, however, looked upon more importantly in some countries than others.

A letter of reservation may be sent when the Master has reservations concerning the accuracy of information supplied by another party. The need for such a letter may arise, for example, when the amount of cargo claimed to have been discharged by cargo interests is less than the amount determined by the ship's own calculations or from an outturn draught survey.

In all instances where a letter of protest or reservation has been sent by the Master, a copy should also be sent to the shipowner and charterer. If the situation warrants it, the Master should not hesitate to call for further assistance from the shipowners or the P&I Club at the time of an incident.

4.4.15. Mitigation

The concept of mitigation is basically involved with minimising or reducing the consequences of an incident after it has arisen.

In most cases, if the correct action is taken immediately after an incident occurs, then considerable extra damage, losses and expenses can be avoided.

To some extent it may be possible to develop contingency plans for mitigation purposes—e.g. with regard to oil spills or a fire etc. It is not so easy, perhaps, to anticipate what might happen during the loading, carrying or discharge of innumerable different cargoes, but some forethought would be well rewarded.

It may be tempting to ignore a problem and hope that no-one else notices. It is suggested that this would be a serious mistake. A vigilant cargo watch should be maintained and, if a problem is detected, then it should be dealt with immediately, whether it be separating wet, damaged grain from the rest of the bulk or stopping loading a product cargo if it is discovered that the wrong valve has been opened etc.

Clearly, initial mitigation efforts may have to be done by the Master and crew until the P&I Club correspondent or surveyor, etc., can board the vessel.

4.5.0. Collecting evidence

Legal disputes involving the vessel are amongst the many risks inherent in the business of owning and operating ships. Owners' success in these disputes may depend almost entirely on the availability of contemporaneous evidence from the vessel. In cases where the relevant information and documents are available, claims can usually be resolved quickly, avoiding lengthy legal wrangles and crippling legal costs. In the event that claims are brought before a court or tribunal, judges and arbitrators place great weight upon documentation and other contemporaneous evidence from a vessel. If good, clear, and methodical records are produced the judges and arbitrators will infer that the vessel was operated in a 'seaman-like' manner and more likely to come to a decision in favour of the shipowner.

4.5.1. The Master's role in collecting evidence

The Master and his officers on board ship have a very important role to play in collecting evidence. However, it should never be the intention somehow to expect the Master and his officers to replace lawyers, surveyors and other consultants in assembling evidence. Masters and officers have an independent but no less crucial role to play in the collecting of evidence.

Firstly, they can be of great assistance to lawyers, surveyors, or other consultants instructed by ship owners and their insurers to go on board the vessel to investigate an incident. When an incident occurs a significant period of time may elapse before the lawyer or surveyor is able to come on board the vessel. In that period of time, valuable information may be destroyed or lost inadvertently. The Master and officers can ensure that they gather together all the relevant information and documents for the lawyer or surveyor to examine when they finally arrive. In addition, they can interview witnesses immediately after an incident while memories are still fresh. The assistance of the Master and officers will make the job of the lawyer or surveyor far easier, will save a considerable amount of time, and will go a long way in ensuring that as thorough an investigation as possible is carried out.

Secondly, there are many minor incidents and disputes which arise during the normal course of a vessel's trading. These may not develop into claims for a considerable time after the incident occurred. The cost involved in investigating such claims by engaging lawyers or other consultants are disproportionate to the amount at stake and thus not economically viable. Moreover, although the claims may be relatively small, they tend to arise often and, collectively, they represent a substantial amount of money. Therefore, the information recorded by the Master and officers on a regular and routine basis will be essential in defending these claims.

Finally, an increased awareness of the type of evidence required to defend a claim will also lead to an increased awareness of potential problems which could arise on a vessel and, therefore, could lead to greater care being taken by the Master and officers in operating the vessel.

4.5.2. Evidence in cargo claims

The main objectives of the Hague—Hague Visby Rules is to ensure that the cargo is delivered in like good order and condition which means that the condition of the cargo should not have deteriorated whilst it was in the care and custody of the carrier, however the rules recognise the possibility that, for reasons beyond the control of the carrier, he may fail to meet that obligation.

In such cases, the rules may protect the carrier from liability for claims arising out of this failure to deliver the cargo 'in like good order and condition' (see Hague Visby Rules, Article IV, Rules 1 and 2). However, before he can rely on these exceptions the carrier must fulfil all of his obligations under the rules. The carrier, in seeking to defend a claim for cargo loss or damage, must first demonstrate that he has exercised due diligence to make the ship seaworthy and that he has properly kept and cared for the cargo. If the carrier fails to show that he has fulfilled these obligations, he will not be able to rely on the exceptions.

There are three important points, which must be clearly understood. Firstly, the exceptions will only come to the aid of the carrier if he has done everything possible to look after the cargo and prevent loss or damage occurring. Secondly, the scope of the exceptions are continually diminishing; the carrier is expected to learn not only from his own mistakes but also from those of other carriers within the shipping community. Thirdly, as with the deviation provisions, the exceptions are interpreted in a narrow and restrictive sense and the carrier can never rely on them confidently.

The obligations imposed on the carrier by the rules have been devised to keep loss and damage to a minimum. Thus, it is likely that where cargo loss and damage has arisen the carrier will be found to have been in breach of the rules. That does not mean that the carrier will be found liable for every cargo claim brought against him. However, the carrier will be in a far better position to defend claims and to produce the evidence required to refute them if he has implemented, in the first instance, the very systems and procedures on board the vessel which minimise the risks of claims arising.

In a claim for cargo loss or damage, the documentary evidence should be assembled whenever possible and numbered in consecutive order. *The Masters Role in Collecting Evidence* sets out a non-exhaustive list of documents. The documents should then be referred to in the Master's report. Suggestions on how the Master's report could perhaps be structured and what sort of information could be included is set out in *The Masters Role in Collecting Evidence*. It is recognised that in certain instances these documents will be more easily available from the shipowner's office, but if they are available on the vessel and attached to the report they will be of great assistance in limiting the amount of commentary which has to be included in the report.

4.6.0. Writing reports

One of the important tasks performed by the master is to provide shipowners with up-to-date information concerning the vessel's progress and movement throughout the voyage.

Obviously, some shipowners will require more information from their Masters than others and may even lay down in the Master's standing orders the kind of information they require. A lot of the information sent by the master will be fairly routine, such as advising shipowners of port arrival or departure, bunker or store requirments, confirming vessel is ready to load cargo and so on.

The Master's reports, of concern in this section, are those involving P&I related incidents in general and cargo loss or damage incidents specifically.

In the event of a major incident, lawyers and/or consultants will be engaged to investigate the matter. Part of this investigation will probably involve taking evidence and statements from relevant members of the ship's crew and other possible witnesses.

The Master should co-operate with the lawyer attending on behalf of the shipowner and/or the shipowner's P&I Club and be guided as to what additional reports should be prepared.

The Master should also be on his guard and ensure that the true identity of lawyers and consultants is established, and who they are acting for, before he hands over any evidence, provides access to his vessel or discusses the incident.

It has not been unknown for a Master to hand over all the relevant documentation and evidence and provide very full statements to a lawyer who has attended on board, only to find out later that the lawyer was acting on behalf of claimants!

The rest of the officers and crew should also be warned about talking to strangers and should refer any enquiries to the Master. However, for the smaller incidents or where there is going to be a delay in the lawyers/consultants arriving on board, then it would be appropriate for the Master to prepare a contemporaneous report on the incident.

When the Master prepares his own report, it is vitally important that it is concise, factual, and objective.

At all costs, the Master should avoid introducing into the report opinions or conjecture on what third parties might have been doing. The report may have to be disclosed to the other parties and, if proceedings do take place, opinions may not stand up well under cross examination and, invariably, do not further— and may even prejudice—the shipowner's interests.

The main thing is to keep the report concise, factual and objective and, whenever possible, include sketches and photographs which can be worth a thousand words.

The sort of information which the master should include in the report will clearly be determined by the incident itself and it would not be possible to legislate for every conceivable type of incident. However, *The Masters Role in Collecting Evidence* should provide a guide and a set of suggestions on some of the important aspects and pieces of information which the master should or may care to consider incorporating.

If the Master, in the circumstances, considers an incident will at some stage prejudice the shipowner's position, the report should be prepared in anticipation of litigation, marked confidential and addressed to the shipowner's lawyers.

If the dominant purpose of the report being prepared in the first place was in anticipation of litigation, it may not have to be disclosed to other parties.

English arbitration and court proceedings are conducted on the basis that each party to an action submits evidence in support of their case. The general rule is that the parties to the proceedings must disclose and produce all relevant documents. In this context 'disclosed' means that the existence of the documents must be made known. 'Produced' means that they must be made available for inspection.

The one exception to the general rule is that documents which are privileged are exempt from production (although not disclosure). In some other jurisdictions, the rules in relation to production of all relevant documents are even stricter than in England.

A Master's report is relevant to legal proceedings and may be used by the other parties to the proceedings as evidence, unless it is privileged. The report may be privileged on the grounds of legal professional privilege or on the grounds that it is a self-incriminating document.

For a more detailed discussion of the doctrine of privilege, please see *The Masters Role in Collecting Evidence* book, p7.ff.

5.0.0. CONCLUSIONS

At the end of the day, then, we are left with something of a problem. Few would argue that the level of claims and, as a consequence, the insurance premiums are too high. Many different factors have been identified as contributing to the problem but in almost every case, the cause of the loss or damage can be reduced to a human error or at least a human element.

For economic reasons there has been a significant change in the identity of officers and crew who man the merchant ships of today compared with a decade ago, accompanied by a serious breakdown in the relationship between the shipowners as employer and the sea staff as employees. It may be just a coincidence that this has occurred at exactly the same time that claims started to escalate at an alarming rate; maybe not! Further economy measures, in addition to employing fewer and cheaper crews, which have been undertaken during the last decade or so, were to cut back to an absolute minimum (and beyond that in some cases) on essential maintenance and to keep the ships trading long past and age they would normally have been scrapped. It has been shown however that the result of these so-called 'economy' measures has been to force insurance premiums up by more than 300% in many cases in a period of about six years, because of a rising incidence of claims. Such that in some cases a shipowner is spending almost half of his total operating budget on insurance costs.

It would seem therefore, that the claims problem can be reduced to a human problem but it can probably be reduced further to an economic problem.

In the title to this paper, it is suggested that there was going to be put forward a NEW approach to loss prevention—that was not to be. The suggestion is that we try to turn the clock backwards and rebuild the relationships which used to exist between the shipowner and the Master, officers and crew—of whatever nationality. Only then can progress be made with such things as loss prevention, training courses etc. The question we should be asking is how can this be done and also whether or not it is too late to do anything about it. There is certainly a serious shortage of properly qualified officers and crew around the world and this is forecast to get worse. Little training has been carried out in the traditional maritime countries during the last ten or 15 years—indeed many of the nautical training establishments have closed down.

But to shipowners pockets are not very deep in such difficult market conditions. Invariably, it is the shipowner who has the finger pointed at him and on whose doorstep the blame is laid. However, we should think a little more carefully about this matter. The shipowner does not have sufficient funds to employ a large highly qualified, well experienced and highly motivated crew, to maintain the ship in perfect first class condition, to replace with a new building at twelve years of age, because the amount of hire or freight they are receiving from the charterers or shippers is too low. The hire and freight rates are too low because national governments insist on keeping inflation low and the end consumer—the final purchaser is not prepared to pay more for his goods. The price of goods—and inflation is kept low because the shipowner is prepared to carry goods for a cripplingly low rate of return. As far as cargo loss and damage is concerned, which is the subject of this paper, then the public tends to remain blissfully ignorant of the problem because they are not directly affected. However, when a major stranding or pollution incident occurs, there is mass media and public hysteria—although within a few weeks of the incident they return to their blissful ignorance. Whether we are discussing pollution incidents or collisions or cargo loss or damage the underlying problem is very similar.

There has to be self regulation within the industry—if not, then others will surely legislate for the shipping industry—and a more favourable climate must be established to help the shipowners make an investment in people, contemplate scrapping older tonnage and consider new buildings even if this does mean, at the end of the day, paying more for one's petrol or bananas or aluminium pans or whatever.

In the meantime, we must all do our best to encourage sea staff and shore staff to work towards avoiding or minimising claims as best they can and it is hoped that much of what has been said in this paper will help towards that end or will help to provide a better understanding of what sort of information and evidence those ashore dealing with claims require from the ship and what sort of documentation etc. can be produced from the ship.

In the hope that this small contribution will help towards a solution of the problem.

TALLY SCHEDULE - BAGGED CARGOES

Cargo.

a. Is the shipment
- [ ] break-bulk
- [ ] palletised
- [ ] pre-slung

b. Is the loading/discharge by
- [ ] separate bags
- [ ] nets
- [ ] slings
- [ ] pallets

c. Is the loading/discharge
- [ ] continuous over 24 hour periods

Tallying Operation.

1. Tally Clerk Arrangements.

a. Where are the tally clerks located ie
- [x] hold
- [x] deck
- [x] jetty

b. Is there one tally clerk
- [ ] per stevedore gang
- [ ] per hold

c. Are tally clerks working regular shifts [ ]

Are the tally clerks changed after each shift [ ]

2. Counting Arrangements.

a. What is being counted i.e.
- [ ] bags
- [ ] slings
- [ ] nets
- [ ] pallets
- [ ] trucks

b. Are tally clerks present
- [ ] all the time

if not, how is the tally maintained

....

....

c. Give details of examples of tally clerk negligence i.e.
- [ ] absence
- [ ] inattention
- [ ] sleeping
- [ ] confusion

3. Tally Sheets and Figures

a. Are daily tally sheets presented for signature on completion
- [ ] each day
- [ ] each shift

Is the vessel able to sign and enter remarks [ ]

b. Is the final outturn tally figure presented for signature [ ]

Is the vessel able to sign and enter remarks* [ ]

4. Damaged Bags

a. How were the bags damaged ie
- [ ] stevedores (hooks/bad handling)
- [ ] falling from slings

b. Are torn and slack bags being tallied [ ]

c. Are sweepings and refilled bags being tallied [ ]

d. Are the tally figures for these being presented to the vessel for signature [ ]
and can remarks be entered [ ]

Making Protests Count as Evidence

In the event the vessel is dissatisfied with the tallying arrangements, an immediate protest should be made, which should be:-

a. Specific in describing the complaint being made ie insufficient tally clerks per hold tally clerks sleeping and/or absent from post daily/shift tally figures not presented for signature and entering of remarks

b. Dated and signed by master and/or chief officer

c. Separate copies addressed to tally clerk supervisor, receiver and agent whose signatures should be obtained on the vessel's copy

d. Backed up with a log entry and complemented with survey report compiled by master or chief officer.

*Absence of Final Outturn Tally and/or Certificate.

In the event that the final tally figure and/or outturn report is not made available to the vessel, a protest should be made. This should be backed up with a formal letter of instruction given to the agent to ensure that, when the tally and report is eventually presented to the agent for signature, the agent enters appropriate remarks to protect the shipowner's interests.

☑ = "yes" or "this category"   ☒ = "no"

Note: Photographs taken by crew members will strengthen the vessel's own documentary evidence to protect against inadequate tallying operations and loss/damage to cargo, when used to accompany log entries, notes of protest, master's reports and remarks in tally sheets or outturn reports.

Produced by **The North of England P. & I. Association Ltd.**, 2-8 Fenkle Street, Newcastle upon Tyne. NE1 5DS.
Telephone: 091 232 5221 Telex: NEPIA G 53634/537316 Fax: 091 261 0540
Should you require further copies please contact **Graham Anderson** at the Association.